LINCOLN CHRISTIAN UNIVERSITY

101

school success tools
for smart kids with
Learning
Difficulties

101

school success tools
for smart kids with

Learning
Difficulties

**Betty Roffman Shevitz, Marisa Stemple,
Linda Barnes-Robinson, and Sue Jeweler**

PRUFROCK PRESS INC.
WACO, TEXAS

Library of Congress Cataloging-in-Publication Data

101 school success tools for smart kids with learning difficulties / Betty Roffman Shevitz ... [et al.].
    p. cm.
  Includes bibliographical references.
  ISBN 978-1-59363-533-6 (pbk.)
  1. Learning disabled children--Education. 2. Learning disabled children--Identification. 3. Gifted children--Education. 4.
  Motivation in education. I. Roffman Shevitz, Betty, 1954- II. Title: One hundred one school success tools for smart kids with learn-
  ing difficulties. III. Title: One hundred and one school success tools for smart kids with learning difficulties.
  LC4704.A15 2011
  371.95'6--dc22
                         2010053501

Edited by Lacy Compton

Cover Design by Marjorie Parker

Layout Design by Raquel Trevino

ISBN-13: 978-1-59363-533-6

Prufrock Press Inc.
P.O. Box 8813
Waco, TX 76714-8813
Phone: (800) 998-2208
Fax: (800) 240-0333
http://www.prufrock.com

Dedications

To all of the kids who taught us everything we wanted to know and more, and to the teachers who work so hard every day to "turn on the bright" in their students.

To my husband, Max; my sons, Michael and Andy; my mother, Gloria; and my sister, Sally; and in memory of my father.

To my husband, Ronnie, and my wonderful parents, Erna and Richard.

To Art, my children, and my grandchildren.

To Larry, Brie, and Alexis.

Contents

List of Tools

Introduction

HAVE you ever had students in your classroom who just confused you because they struggled with many classroom activities, yet seemed so smart at the same time? Maybe you have had a student who couldn't read, but knocked your socks off whenever it was time for a science lesson or lab. Or perhaps you have had a student who read like an adult but was unable to spell and hated to write. Or maybe you have had a student who appeared to be "average," but every once in a while you would see a spark of brilliance and wonder what else you had been missing. If so, this book is for you! These are the students who we refer to as "smart kids with learning difficulties," and this book is devoted to helping you find them, teach them, and nurture their potential.

Meet Some Smart Kids With Learning Difficulties

"Sarah has so many great ideas in class discussions, but when I ask her to write responses about what she has read, I get little if anything on paper. I wish I could help her get her ideas down—I know she is bright. Is she lazy?"

"Whenever anyone has a question about history, whether it is Ancient Civilizations or the American Revolution, Jeremy is our resident expert, spouting off detailed accounts of periods in history, yet he has trouble working cooperatively in groups. I don't get it."

"Darryl's mother and science teacher constantly tell me how bright he is, but frankly, I just don't see it! He seems like just an average kid who is doing fine."

You know them—bright kids sitting in your classes who are struggling because they have learning difficulties that interfere with their ability to be successful. Some are easy to spot, and you are immediately aware of their difficulty in reading, writing, organization, or memory. Some really smart students just seem unmotivated, yet you wonder if there is an underlying reason for this apparent "laziness." Then there are kids like Darryl, who appear average, because their difficulties and gifts are masking each other, but who are actually anything but average. In all of these cases, their gifts and talents are hidden—waiting to be revealed by the skillful teacher who knows how and where to look, and then knows what to do to help these students be successful.

Bright kids who are not reaching their potential present themselves in different ways, depending on what is contributing to their lack of success and achievement. The social/emotional well-being of children is a prime factor in their readiness to learn. Gifted students with learning difficulties typically experience symptoms of worry and sadness related to their school frustration. Therefore, addressing the social/emotional needs of these students is a critical factor in educating them and helping them to reach their full potential. The lesson may be outstanding and the teacher may be terrific, but if the young person is socially and/or emotionally not available, the learning will suffer.

There are many reasons why students may be underperforming in school and various disabilities that may be impacting their level of productivity. *101 School Success Tools for Smart Kids With Learning Difficulties* is not "disorder specific" in its design and is not meant to be a diagnostic tool. The goal of this book is not to label, but rather to help teachers gain an understanding of who these students are, what struggles they face, and how best to address their needs so they may develop intellectually, socially, and emotionally.

101 School Success Tools for Smart Kids With Learning Difficulties provides you with tools and strategies to help you recognize and nurture the potential in these students. As the teacher, you are in the position to be able to serve as a catalyst, empowering these students to become successful learners. As you discover the types of learners they are, you will be able to help them work through their strengths, understand their needs, and begin to realize their true potential. As you help your students learn more about themselves, they will gain confidence and independence, and ultimately translate their knowledge into plans and strategies that will enable them to be successful in school.

Although parents may be the first to recognize their children's gifts and learning difficulties, your role is critical in ensuring that students receive the challenge and support they need. It is a varied role that moves fluidly from educator, interpreter, facilitator, manager, motivator, guide, director, and advo-cate, while ensuring that the learning environment is the best it can be. With the necessary resources and a thorough understanding of these students, you determine a precise educational direction and create a dynamic program that helps to "turn on the bright."

How to Use This Book

The information in the book is cumulative in nature. On the next two pages is a graphic organizer, provided as a way to record your thinking as you read and reflect on the information in each chapter. The first part of the organizer is a K-W-L template, a strategy often used with students (Ogle, 1986). You may find it a practical and relevant tool for your own learning as well. The second part of the graphic organizer is called the Transfer/Application Template and is designed for you to record your thoughts and plans based on what you have learned in each chapter. If you find this organizer helpful, we encourage you to reproduce it to use for each succeeding chapter.

We ask that you avoid the urge to skip the chapter overviews (as we all find ourselves doing from time to time) as the content addresses the guid-ing questions, providing valuable information and detailed rationale for the tools that follow. Each overview opens with a set of Guiding Questions and Word Sparks, key words found within the chapter. These two components are designed to activate your knowledge and develop your ideas as you read through the materials. In addition, each chapter also revisits Sarah, Jeremy, and Darryl to illustrate the information provided. After reading the overview, review the tools in the chapter, selecting those that best meet your needs and the needs of your student(s). The tools and tips (insights into the use of the tools) are designed to help you in your instructional planning for these students. Some pages are designed to use directly with the students, either one-on-one, in a small group, or with your whole class, while others provide you with tools to help with your instructional planning or to further develop your professional knowledge. We are aware that the tools for students are in a paper-and-pencil format and that the kids that they are designed to serve are the very ones who may require alternative products that reflect their understanding of concepts and content material. Therefore, as you study the tools and plan for their use, realize that student responses may need to be dictated or recorded. For your convenience, the publisher has also made all of the student tools accessible through its website using the link: http://www.prufrock.com/skld.

As you are working with your students and are beginning to unmask their gifts, remember to seek out their parents as a resource. Parents are a child's first teachers and can provide information on strengths and gifts that may not be evident in your classroom. For this reason, each chapter includes tools called

KWL Template

What I Know	What I Want to Know	What I Learned

Transfer/Application Template

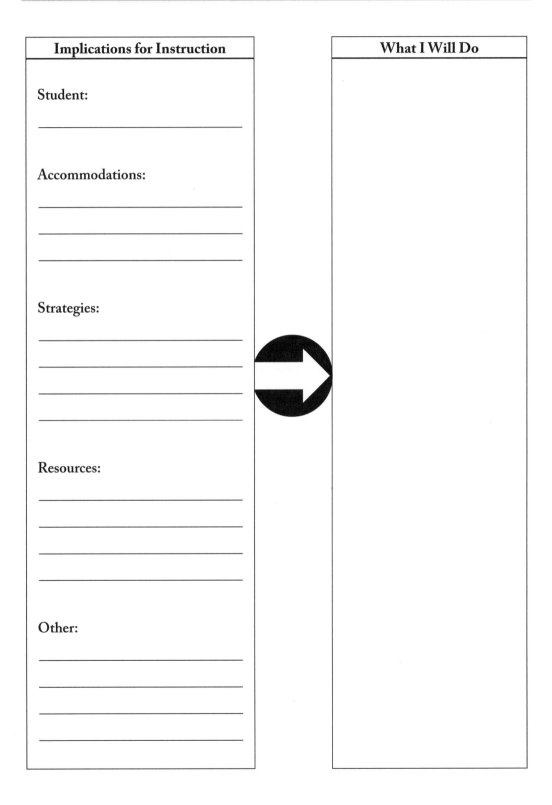

Implications for Instruction	What I Will Do
Student: _____	
Accommodations: _____ _____ _____	
Strategies: _____ _____ _____ _____	
Resources: _____ _____ _____ _____	
Other: _____ _____ _____ _____	

Parent Partnership Pieces to share with parents that complement the teaching tools and tips. Some of the activities are designed to help parents recognize strengths in their child or better understand ways to support his or her needs. Others draw on the parents' own expertise and knowledge of their children and provide an opportunity for parents to share information with you about their children that may not be evident in the classroom.

At the end of each chapter, following the tools, is a list of additional ideas for Keeping the Bright Turned On. We hope that by progressing through the book at your own pace, you will have a meaningful learning experience and truly have an impact on the bright students with learning difficulties in your class. Although we know that all students will certainly benefit from the best practices included in this book, these students *need* these components to survive. Experience tells us that turning on the bright requires working together to gain a better understanding of who these students are. This is their best hope for success. Key to this success is the teacher's and parents' adoption of the firm belief that these students are gifted first and challenged by learning difficulties second. Only then will students learn to see themselves as successful learners because they understand who they are and what they need.

Now it is time to turn on the bright!

chapter 1

Who Are These Kids?

No bird soars too high if he soars with his own wings.
—Ralph Waldo Emerson

Guiding Questions

❏ Who is included in this population?
❏ What are the characteristics of smart kids with learning difficulties?

Word Sparks

✓ characteristics
✓ twice-exceptional
✓ gifted
✓ strengths
✓ weaknesses
✓ disability

✓ IEP
✓ 504 Plan
✓ profile
✓ impairments
✓ social-emotional

Chapter Overview

IN today's world, our classrooms are diverse and our students have varied abilities, interests, skills, and backgrounds. Although there are now rigorous academic standards that all children must attain, educators realize the importance of adjusting instruction so that *every* student can learn and grow. In the case of a gifted student with learning difficulties, this may mean adjusting instruction "up" and "down" and sometimes laterally within one unit, one lesson, and even within a single activity. It means increasing the challenge for these students while simultaneously increasing the supports. This is a complex maneuver for a teacher of many students to accomplish, but with the right knowledge, resources, and tools, it is possible! And when done well, the rewards are visible and infinite. A child can be transformed from a student who says, "I'm stupid," and who dreads school, to a student who says, "I'm smart, but I learn differently," and who loves learning. In order to appropriately adjust instruction to meet the needs of our bright students with learning difficulties, we first need to know who they are as learners.

Who Are These Kids?

Bright kids with learning difficulties are twice-exceptional students who are advanced in at least one way and simultaneously possess learning challenges. They may or may not be formally recognized as gifted or officially identified with a disability, and they may or may not have a formal educational plan such as an Individualized Education Program (IEP) or 504 Plan. If recognized as a student with a disability, the category or label may vary. Many twice-exceptional students with learning challenges have a learning disability (LD) in reading and/or writing and struggle to acquire basic academic skills. Others may be diagnosed with Attention Deficit/Hyperactivity Disorder (ADHD) and have difficulty with attention, organization, and production. Additionally, autism spectrum disorders such as Asperger's syndrome, high-functioning autism, or Pervasive Developmental Disorder-Not Otherwise Specified (PDD-NOS) often coexist with above-average or gifted ability. Still others may have vision impairments, hearing loss, physical disabilities, or other disorders. Some twice-exceptional students have more than one recognized disability or have a "fuzzy" profile where they have many characteristics typical of different diagnoses, making the designation of one label difficult. We also know that students with the same label can be different and that labeling a student's disability does not tell us what to do about it. While under federal and state laws and regulations, it is often a necessary part of the process to identify and label the disability; the important thing in this book is not the label, but the understanding of the student as an individual with a unique array of strengths and weaknesses.

Bright students with learning difficulties often confound teachers because they have significant strengths and surprising weaknesses. They are often incredibly articulate and verbal, but simultaneously have production problems and may be significantly impacted in the areas of written output, organization, memory, reading, attention, and social skills. Many times these students seem average because the gifts and the learning difficulties are masking one another. There are also students who, despite a lack of any documented disability, are underachieving. These students are often the most difficult to understand and reach because they do not fall into a neat category with specific instructional skills that can be addressed.

Social/Emotional Characteristics

Regardless of category or label, bright students with learning difficulties often do not understand why they have so much difficulty at school. They are told that they are smart by the adults in their lives, but they may feel "dumb" when they compare their ability to read, write, organize, or socialize with the "smart" kids at school. Can you imagine how you would feel if you had so many creative ideas and good information to share, but could not write fast enough or well enough to get these ideas on paper? Bright students with learning difficulties generally want to please their teachers and produce quality work, but many have difficulty with starting or finishing a task. They often struggle to keep up with classroom expectations, causing many of these students to feel extremely frustrated and anxious. They may avoid schoolwork because of these feelings of inadequacy and develop problematic behaviors (e.g., frequent trips to the bathroom or nurse, work avoidance, task negotiations) in an attempt to hide or escape their weaknesses. Other common signs of emotional distress that parents may see are the student crying or making self-deprecating comments, not wanting to go to school, and refusing to do homework. These behaviors often can be clues that there is something wrong and may be signs of a possible learning problem, particularly if they occur *only* when the student is asked to read or write. A skilled teacher will analyze the behavior to determine why it is occurring.

There are two characteristics that are important to discuss, as they are pervasive in gifted children (with and without disabilities): perfectionism and emotional overexcitability. Perfectionism is a combination of thoughts and behaviors associated with high expectations for one's own performance. Kids with perfectionism often would prefer to take an incomplete, even if it meant their teacher thought they didn't care, rather than hand in something that didn't meet their own expectations. In the case of gifted students with learning difficulties, this perfectionism coupled with lower performance translates into work avoidance, work destruction, and what is often described by teachers as "shutting down" or disengaging from the learning process. One cannot fail at something one does not try. This is an unfortunate lesson that many of these students learn early on as they experience school failure relative to their own expectations.

Emotional overexcitability refers to an emotional sensitivity and richness in creatively and intellectually gifted children that is characterized by strong emotions and reactions to their inner conflict between the world as it is and the world as they believe it should be (Dabrowski, 1964). The work of Dabrowski (1964) and Piechowski (1991) suggested that the higher levels of developmental potential in the gifted sometimes create crises characterized by strong emotions, and these strong emotional reactions are a critical part of developing the personalities of gifted children. Overexcitabilities represent a real difference in the fabric of life and quality of experience for these students. Parents often notice emotional overexcitability first. It is reflected in heightened, intense feelings; extremes of complex emotions; identification with others' feelings; and strong affective expression (Piechowski, 1991). Gifted and learning-disabled (GT/LD) kids may manifest these overexcitability behaviors to an even greater degree because of their struggle to be recognized as being bright or gifted, and therefore often having their needs unmet.

Student Profiles

Let's revisit the students we met in the introduction and explore their characteristics further.

Sarah

Sarah is able to comprehend advanced mathematics concepts, yet is unable to show her work or organize her materials. She is a strong reader and loves science fiction. She has a strong imagination and is often "in her own world," coming up with fantastical stories and ideas. She can decode text well above grade level; however, she has difficulty attending to, and therefore comprehending, text that she is not particularly interested in reading (teacher-assigned text). She demonstrates good spelling and a grasp of punctuation and capitalization on weekly quizzes, yet her own writing is full of mechanical errors. She can talk at length about almost anything, but she struggles to organize her ideas in writing. She has trouble selecting a topic from all of the ideas swimming around in her head, and once she picks one, she has trouble figuring out what to say first. Most often, she sits "thinking" while the other kids are writing and her pieces are rarely completed. When finished, they are short and to the point, failing to represent her creative and complex ideas. Sarah is hopelessly disorganized. She forgets to bring home her books for her homework and forgets to return completed assignments back to school. She loses papers almost as soon as she is given them. Sarah seems to have no internal clock. It takes her forever to get started on her work, and she often saves things for the last minute, not realizing how much time it will take to accomplish the task. Sarah says she wants to be more organized, but she never wants to use her teacher's methods for organizing her time or materials, saying she likes *her* system better.

Jeremy

Jeremy has more background knowledge about the next social studies unit than anyone else in the class. He has an amazing vocabulary, and his memory for facts and details is astounding! He can identify all of the U.S. presidents, the dates they held office, and the names of their vice presidents. He is strong overall in mathematics. He is a good reader and understands advanced nonfiction text easily, but he has a hard time understanding the deeper meaning of stories, as he doesn't connect easily to the thoughts and feelings of the characters. He also struggles with the nonliteral language often found in fiction such as similes, metaphors, words with multiple meanings, and idioms and proverbs. He can answer factual questions about text easily, but responds in a limited fashion to interpretive or evaluative questions. Jeremy has poor fine motor skills and has a hard time getting his ideas on paper. He wants to have friends but is socially awkward. He has difficulty reading social cues and doesn't seem to know the rules of conversational language, and therefore doesn't connect with his peers. During group work, Jeremy sits off to the side and does not participate. He seems very anxious most of the time. He dislikes sudden noises, crowds of people, and being touched. Jeremy needs structure and predictability to perform well in the classroom, as he has a hard time with transitions and unexpected changes. When he is overwhelmed or upset, he sometimes has very disruptive meltdowns and can become inconsolable and aggressive. Overall, he is a very sweet and smart boy.

Darryl

Darryl is fascinated with dinosaurs, sharks, and engineering. He watches the Discovery Channel all of the time and loves to build intricate structures with his LEGOs™. He has incredible problem-solving skills and demonstrates strong reasoning ability. He grasps very advanced concepts in science and social studies quickly when they are presented orally or visually. He has an amazing vocabulary and is incredibly articulate. Watching Darryl give an oral presentation is like watching a little professor. Darryl is able to listen to and discuss very advanced and complex text in a reading discussion, yet he is unable to decode even simplistic, below-grade-level text. He reads slowly and with many errors and this impacts his comprehension of text read independently. Darryl's mathematical reasoning is advanced, yet he does not know his basic math facts despite Herculean efforts to drill them into his memory. A great source of frustration for Darryl is his abysmal handwriting and spelling, as he has so many ideas he wants to share in his writing but is physically unable to do so. Darryl has lots of friends and is athletic and artistic. Some of his teachers see how smart he is, but Darryl often says he feels stupid.

Hopefully, reading about these students has helped to illustrate the characteristics of bright students with learning difficulties. You probably have students in your class right now who resemble these students. Or maybe Sarah, Jeremy, and Darryl remind you of students from past years that you wish you had better understood. This means that you are building the ability to recognize the pattern of strengths and weaknesses that would signal that a student is smart and has learning difficulties.

What else can we learn from these student profiles? These students are all different and yet they have something in common. They all have a scattered profile of extreme strengths and significant weaknesses. Some advanced abilities come very easily to them while other skills are hard for them. One way to understand the profile of bright students with learning difficulties like Sarah, Jeremy, and Darryl is to think of the phrase, "The hard things are easy and the easy things are hard." Things that are easy for the average student to learn (e.g., basic reading skills, simple writing tasks, recalling math facts, organizing papers) often are hard for twice-exceptional students to master, but things that are hard for most students (e.g., interpretive understanding of literature, creating unique ideas and stories, finding new ways to solve difficult math problems) come very naturally to them. Smart kids with learning difficulties can't do many of the things that average students their age can easily do, yet they are beyond their peers in many ways conceptually, cognitively, and intellectually.

Conclusion

Understanding these students is a complex but critical task, as it helps us to understand the struggles they face, address their needs, and support their intellectual, social, and emotional development. Smart kids with learning difficulties often go unrecognized and thus do not receive the challenging instruction or supports that they need to be successful. But you *can* learn to recognize the strengths and weaknesses within students and identify these students in your classroom. The tools presented in this chapter will support you as you undertake the tasks of understanding the characteristics of these students and increasing your ability to spot them in your classroom. As with all of the tools in this book, feel free to use, modify, or adapt them according to your needs.

Recognizing the strengths and weaknesses within the individual is the first step toward reaching and teaching these students. Once the student's strengths and needs are known, the teacher must then make appropriate instructional decisions for the student that take into consideration his gifts and obstacles.

Exploring the question, "Who are these kids?" may help shape the attitudes of teachers and parents regarding the presence of the strengths, gifts, talents, interests, and challenges inherent in each child.

Tool 1:
Parent Partnership Piece
Introductory Letter

Parents are an invaluable resource to you. By working together you will be able to gain a better understanding of who these students are, as their strengths are not always evident in the classroom.

Tips

- ✓ *Tool 1: Parent Partnership Piece: Introductory Letter.* Use this letter, or one similar to it, as an introduction to your parents about turning on the bright as one of your goals for the year.
- ✓ Each chapter includes at least one Parent Partnership Piece that provides information on what you are doing with their child, gives the parents opportunity to share information with you, and provides a way for parents to build on concepts that you have introduced to their child.
- ✓ You may find that some of the pieces are relevant to all of your parents while others might be more appropriate for parents of smart kids with learning difficulties.

Tool 1: Parent Partnership Piece

Tool 1: Parent Partnership Piece
Introductory Letter

Dear Parent,

Every person has his or her strengths as an individual. One of my goals this year is to help your child *turn on the bright*—discover and develop his or her individual strengths. I hope to help your child learn more about who he or she is as a learner, what his or her strengths are, and how he or she learns best, because the more a child understands about his or her strengths and areas of need, the better chance that he or she will be successful in school. To do this, I need your help.

Throughout the year, we will be doing activities that help your child develop a strong concept of who he or she is. We will be focusing on his or her strengths, what defines him or her as a learner, what ways he or she learns best, and how to advocate for him- or herself. As your child's first teacher, you play an integral role in this process. For this reason, from time to time, I will be sending home a Parent Partnership Piece to inform you of what we have discussed in class and provide you with the opportunity to share things about your child that may not be evident in school.

I look forward to working with you to gain a better understanding of who your child is and how to help him or her have a successful year. If you have any questions or suggestions, please feel free to contact me.

Sincerely,

Tools 2 and 3: Characteristics Charts

Often misunderstood, students with gifts who also have learning challenges that affect their performance are sometimes regarded as lazy or apathetic because educators frequently do not have knowledge about the characteristics of this unique and rare population. Although the strengths and weaknesses of these students vary greatly from student to student, there are some general commonalities that you can begin to look for within your students.

Tips

✓ *Tool 2: Characteristics of Gifted Students With and Without Learning Difficulties.* Observe your students. Reproduce the chart and, using the blank column, list students in your class who exhibit these characteristics. If you find that there are students whose names come up several times on the chart, then you may want to flag these students as ones to watch.

✓ *Tool 3: Parent Partnership Piece: That's My Kid!* Reproduce the chart from Tool 2 and share it with your parents as appropriate.

Tool 2: Characteristics of Gifted Students With and Without Learning Difficulties

Characteristics of Gifted Students Without Learning Difficulties	Characteristics of Gifted Students With Learning Difficulties	Observations/Notes
Ability to learn basic skills quickly and easily and retain information with less repetition	Often struggle to learn basic skills; need to learn compensatory strategies in order to acquire basic skills and information	
High verbal ability	High verbal ability but extreme difficulty in written language area; may use language in inappropriate ways and at inappropriate times	
Early reading ability	Frequently have reading problems	
Keen powers of observation	Strong observation skills but often have deficits in memory skills	
Strong critical thinking, problem-solving, and decision-making skills	Excel in solving real-world problems; outstanding critical thinking and decision-making skills; often independently develop compensatory skills	
Long attention span; persistent, intense concentration	Frequently have attention problems but may concentrate for long periods in areas of interest	
Questioning attitudes	Strong questioning attitudes; may appear disrespectful when questioning information and facts presented by teacher	

Tools 2 and 3: Characteristics Charts

Tools 2 and 3: Characteristics Charts

Creative in the generation of thoughts, ideas, actions; innovative	Unusual imagination; frequently generate original and at times rather bizarre ideas; extremely divergent in thought; may appear to daydream when generating ideas	
Take risks	Often unwilling to take risks with regard to academics; take risks in nonschool areas without consideration of consequences	
Unusual, often highly developed sense of humor	Humor may be used to divert attention from school failure; may use humor to make fun of peers or to avoid trouble	
May mature at different rates than age peers	Sometimes appear immature because they may use anger, crying, withdrawal, and other emotions to express feelings and to deal with difficulties	
Sense of independence	Require frequent teacher support and feedback in weakness areas; highly independent in other areas; often appear to be extremely stubborn and inflexible	
Sensitive	Sensitive regarding weaknesses; highly critical of self and others including teachers; can express concerns about the feelings of others even while engaging in antisocial behavior	

May not be accepted by other children and may feel isolated	May not be accepted by other children and may feel isolated; may be perceived as loners because they do not fit the typical model for either a gifted or a learning disabled student; sometimes have difficulty being accepted by peers due to poor social skills	
Exhibit leadership ability	Exhibit leadership ability; often serve as leaders among the more nontraditional students; demonstrate strong streetwise behavior; the difficulties may interfere with the ability to exercise leadership skills	
Wide range of interests	Wide range of interests but are limited in pursuing them due to learning problems	
Very focused interests (i.e., a passion about certain topics to the exclusion of others)	Very focused interests (i.e., a passion about certain topics to the exclusion of others) often not related to school subjects	

Note. From *Comparison of Characteristics of Gifted Students With or Without Disabilities*, by D. Higgins, L. Baldwin, & D. Pereles, 2000, Unpublished manuscript. Adapted with permission of the authors.

Tools 2 and 3: Characteristics Charts

Tool 3: Parent Partnership Piece
That's My Kid!

Dear Parent,

As we've discussed, your child is very bright and also has some learning challenges. I would like to get more information from you about your child so that I can better understand his or her strengths and needs.

Review the Characteristics of Students With and Without Learning Difficulties chart for characteristics that you may have observed in your child at home. As you read through the characteristics, you might want to jot your observations and notes in the third column. I encourage you to return a copy of your notes to me, or we can set up a time to discuss your observations. The information will be invaluable to me as I plan for your child's success.

Sincerely,

Tools 4–7:
Famous People With
Learning Difficulties

Are there other people like me who are smart but also have learning problems? How did they overcome these obstacles? These tools are designed to help your students answer these questions by learning about famous people who overcame their learning difficulties. Your students (and their parents) may realize that they are bright and still have difficulties at the same time. Or they may not feel smart or be aware of their strengths and weaknesses. Learning about well-known individuals who also experienced learning difficulties provides inspiration for kids, their parents, and their teachers. Infuse the theme of overcoming challenges throughout your instruction. For example, in reading class, analyze a character in a literary piece who has learning challenges. In science class, feature a scientist who overcame obstacles to make his or her discovery.

Tips

✓ *Tool 4: Student Tool: They Did It! So Can I!* Read and discuss the profiles of a few famous people who overcame their learning challenges with your class, in small groups, or with individuals. Additional profiles can be found in *Smart Kids With Learning Difficulties* (Weinfeld, Barnes-Robinson, Jeweler, & Roffman Shevitz, 2006).

✓ *Tool 5: Student Tool: Famous People Who Overcame Learning Challenges.* Have students research a person of interest. This can be an enrichment project or you can combine this idea into a curriculum unit or existing research project. Help students recognize that people with challenges have great potential for success.

✓ *Tool 6: Student Tool: They Can Do It!* Use this template to guide student research. Work with the student to select a person to research, to develop their research questions, to develop a method for note taking, and to make a plan for a product that will help them show what they know through their strengths. Keep in mind that bright students with learning difficulties often prefer to develop their own processes for note taking (e.g., electronic graphic organizers, highlighters, sticky notes).

✓ *Tool 7: Parent Partnership Piece: They Did It! So Can I!* Reproduce Tool 4 and attach it to this letter to help parents work with their child to heighten awareness that people do overcome challenges.

Tool 4: Student Tool
They Did It! So Can I!

She didn't speak at all until she was almost 4 and showed her frustration by screaming and making other noises. She was diagnosed with autism and was considered "weird" by her schoolmates. She had a strong interest in science and a passion for animals and ultimately cultivated her talents into a successful career as a livestock-handling equipment designer. She is also a well-known author who has written many books that help others to understand what it is like to have autism. An award-winning movie was made about her life story. Her compassion, ingenuity, and success have made her a source of inspiration for children with autism and all people. She is Temple Grandin, an author, professor, and advocate.

He was diagnosed with ADHD when he was 9 years old. He had a lot of trouble concentrating in the classroom. He loved swimming and benefitted from the structure it provided and the self-discipline it taught him. He has said, "You can't put a limit on anything. The more you dream, the farther you get." By the age of 25, he held 39 world records and had won 16 Olympic medals. He is Michael Phelps, world-champion swimmer.

He was unable to read until he was 12 years old, and his writing skills were poor throughout his life. In school his mind often wandered and he was terrible at math. He got in trouble a lot because he did not listen when his teachers talked. He has said, "I have not failed. I've just found 10,000 ways that won't work." His ability to think creatively combined with his determination to persist beyond failure helped him to become a famous inventor, and at the time of his death, he held 1,093 patents. He is Thomas Edison, inventor, scientist, and businessman.

She has said, "When I was a kid they didn't call it dyslexia . . . I knew I wasn't stupid, and I knew I wasn't dumb . . . If you read to me, I could tell you everything that you read." She overcame her learning challenges and has had a successful career, being one of very few people to win an Oscar, a Grammy, an Emmy, and a Tony Award. She is Whoopi Goldberg, actress, activist, comedienne, and talk show host.

Tool 5: Student Tool
Famous People Who Overcame Learning Challenges

Directions: Choose a person from the list below and research information about him or her. Create a product that informs an audience about the individual you have studied. You may:

- ✓ write a report,
- ✓ make a storyboard,
- ✓ create a video,
- ✓ perform a skit,
- ✓ create a collage,

- ✓ design a museum exhibit,
- ✓ make a scrapbook,
- ✓ write a song, or
- ✓ design your own product.

Muhammad Ali	Keira Knightley
Hans Christian Anderson	John Lennon
Ann Bancroft (explorer)	Jay Leno
Harry Belafonte	Carl Lewis
Alexander Graham Bell	Greg Louganis
Orlando Bloom	Edward James Olmos
Winston Churchill	Michael Phelps
Bill Cosby	Keanu Reeves
Tom Cruise	Pete Rose
Leonardo da Vinci	Nolan Ryan
Patrick Dempsey	Charles Schwab
Walt Disney	Steven Spielberg
Henry Ford	Quentin Tarantino
Danny Glover	Ted Turner
Whoopi Goldberg	Lindsay Wagner
Salma Hayek	Henry Winkler
Bruce Jenner	Robin Williams
Jewel	Woodrow Wilson
Magic Johnson	

Tool 6: Student Tool
They Can Do It!

Directions: Use pictures or words to capture important or interesting information about your famous person from the Internet, books, or another source.

Name of famous person:		
Biographical information (a chronology of his or her life)	Date	Important or Interesting Event
Strengths this person possessed/ demonstrated		
Weaknesses/ obstacles this person had to overcome		
Important achievements		
Things we have in common		
Things I admire		
How I can use what I have learned?		

Tool 7: Parent Partnership Piece
They Did It! So Can I!

Dear Parent:

In class, we have been reading and discussing profiles of famous people who overcame their learning difficulties. These profiles can provide inspiration for your child, as they help him or her understand that others who we look to as successful role models also experienced learning difficulties. Below are some suggestions of ways that you might use the profiles with your child.

- Use the profiles or a favorite book, TV show, or movie as a springboard to discuss obstacles that the character/famous person learned to overcome. Help your child identify things he or she has in common with that person. For example, "I think you are like_____ because you both_____ and are both good at _____."
- Point out your child's strengths and commend him or her when he or she perseveres to overcome obstacles. Help your child realize that we all have areas in which we excel and areas in which we are not as strong.
- Talk to your child about what is hard about school. Share with him or her about what you found difficult about school, if applicable.
- Ask what your child thinks the teacher or you could do to help him or her succeed in school.

Sincerely,

Tools 8–10:
All About Me!

It is critical to help students focus on their strengths, interests, and talents, rather than on areas that cause them difficulty. These tools will help you gather information about your students and help them build self-confidence and self-esteem.

Tips

✓ *Tool 8: Student Tool: I Can Do It!* Use this tool as a way to gather information about your students and how they view themselves and their strengths.

✓ *Tool 9: Student Tool: Product Preferences.* This tool teaches students that there are a variety of ways that we can show people what we know and helps them establish their product preferences.

✓ *Tool 10: Student Tool: All About Me!* This collage is another opportunity to informally gain information about your students.

Tool 8: Student Tool
I Can Do It!

Directions: As you have learned, many important, successful people faced obstacles that they were able to overcome by using their strengths, interests, and talents. You can, too! On the chart below, circle things that are true about you! Add other ideas to the chart and share this information with your teacher and parents.

Things I Am Good At	Things I Like to Do or Think About	Ways That I Learn Best
Sports Music Art Math Reading Writing Singing	Sports Dinosaurs Music Building things Art Animals Math Science How things work	Watching a video or looking at pictures Doing an experiment Reading it for myself Talking with others Thinking it over on my own Acting it out Singing or listening to songs Building it
Other:	Other:	Other:

Tools 8–10: All About Me!

Tool 9: Student Tool
Product Preferences

Directions: Below are a lot of ways that you can "show what you know." Read over the ideas. Now tell your teacher your preferred ways to express yourself by putting a check by the products that interest you.

I would like to create, plan, or produce a(n):

- ❏ Advertisement
- ❏ Animation
- ❏ Artifact
- ❏ Banner
- ❏ Billboard
- ❏ Book Cover/ Jacket
- ❏ Brochure/Flyer
- ❏ Bulletin Board
- ❏ Calendar
- ❏ Cartoon
- ❏ Chart
- ❏ Collage
- ❏ Collection
- ❏ Comic Book/ Illustrated Story
- ❏ Community Service
- ❏ Computer Program
- ❏ Costume
- ❏ Dance
- ❏ Debate
- ❏ Demonstration
- ❏ Design
- ❏ Diagram
- ❏ Diorama

- ❏ Dramatic Interpretation
- ❏ Drawing
- ❏ Experiment
- ❏ Game
- ❏ Graph
- ❏ Graphic Design
- ❏ Greeting Card
- ❏ Handbook
- ❏ Interview
- ❏ Invention
- ❏ Letter
- ❏ Magazine
- ❏ Map
- ❏ Mime
- ❏ Mobile
- ❏ Mock Trial
- ❏ Model
- ❏ Mural
- ❏ Museum Exhibit
- ❏ Newspaper or News Report
- ❏ Observation Record
- ❏ Opera

- ❏ Outline
- ❏ Painting
- ❏ Petition
- ❏ Photo Essay/ Album
- ❏ Play or Musical
- ❏ Poem
- ❏ Political Cartoon
- ❏ Poster
- ❏ PowerPoint
- ❏ Puppet Show
- ❏ Quilt
- ❏ Role-Play/Skit
- ❏ Scrapbook
- ❏ Sculpture
- ❏ Simulation
- ❏ Song/Rap
- ❏ Speech/Oral Presentation
- ❏ Survey
- ❏ Teach a Lesson
- ❏ TV/Radio Show
- ❏ Video
- ❏ Watercolor
- ❏ Website

Tool 10: Student Tool
All About Me!

Directions: Use the space below or another piece of paper or poster board to express yourself in a collage. Use words, pictures from magazines or the Internet, clip art, photos, or drawings to tell about your personality, things you like and dislike, your interests, things you do well, and things you like to avoid. The more your teacher knows about you, the better!

Tools 8–10: All About Me!

Tool 11:
Ability Olympics

To help students begin to understand who they are as learners, they need to be able to answer the questions "In what ways am I smart?" and "What gets in my way?" Once they can identify their strengths and needs, they can build on their strengths to help circumvent their areas of weakness and know when and where to seek out support.

Tips

✓ *Tool 11: Ability Olympics.* Using the chart, identify several "events" or performance areas on which you want the students to focus (e.g., reading, writing, math, music, arts, sports). Using the Olympic gold medals as the rubric (or create your own), have the students mark their levels of performance in each area. The chart provides a visual of how your students perceive their strengths and areas of need.

✓ You can easily adapt the graphing concept to learning traits or pick a subject area and break it into specific skills. This is important because students often focus on their weaknesses and don't recognize their strengths. For example, under reading, students might list these specific skills: reading words, reading quickly, understanding what I read, understanding what is read to me, and vocabulary. For writing, students might list skills like brainstorming, selecting a topic, spelling, and handwriting.

✓ Date the chart and keep it as a reference, periodically revisiting it to see if students feel they have made any gains in any of the areas. It can be a way for students to chart their progress and see their growth.

✓ Have students customize/individualize their own charts to keep track of their goals.

Tool 11: Student Tool
Ability Olympics

The Events (Performance Areas)					
Gold Medal (My Best Ever)					
Silver Medal (Awesome Effort)					
Bronze medal (Good Job)					
Honorable Mention (In Training)					
Not My Event					

Tool 11: Ability Olympics

Tools 12 and 13: Structured Interviews

One powerful way of gathering information about your students' school experiences and their strengths and weaknesses is to ask them! The puzzle is not complete unless we also ask the parent and the students' other teachers to share their perspectives. In this section, you will find interview questions to help you continue putting the puzzle together.

Tips

✓ *Tool 12: Student Tool: Student Interview.* Use these questions to help you find out more about your students. Don't just give the paper to the students. Ask the questions orally and have them dictate their verbal responses. Ask follow-up questions as needed to probe more deeply. Have your students interview each other so they can find out more about their classmates.

✓ *Tool 13: Parent Partnership Piece: Parent Interview.* Send home the parent interview (or interview the parents over the phone or at a conference). The parents' responses will provide insight that you can use when planning instruction for the student.

Tool 12: Student Tool
Student Interview

1. What do you choose to do in your free time? What are your interests outside of school? What are your hobbies?

   _____

   _____

   _____

   _____

   _____

2. What do you like about school? What are your favorite subjects? Teachers? Activities?

   _____

   _____

   _____

   _____

   _____

3. What do you dislike about school?

   _____

   _____

   _____

   _____

   _____

4. What is easy about school?

   _____

   _____

   _____

   _____

   _____

Tools 12 and 13: Structured Interviews

5. What is difficult about school?

_____

_____

_____

_____

_____

6. If you could change one thing about school, what would you change?

_____

_____

_____

_____

_____

7. What are you really, really good at?

_____

_____

_____

_____

_____

Tool 13: Parent Partnership Piece
Parent Interview

Dear Parent,

We have spent time in class interviewing each other. Interviews are a good way for students to learn about their classmates and for me to learn more about each student. You also are able to provide important information about your child that may increase my understanding of him or her. Please respond to the questions below and return this paper to me or call me to discuss them.

1. What does your child choose to do in his or her free time? What are your child's interests outside of school? What are your child's hobbies?

   _____

   _____

2. What does your child like about school? What are your child's favorite subjects? Teachers? Activities?

   _____

   _____

3. What does your child dislike about school?

   _____

   _____

4. What is easy about school for your child?

   _____

   _____

5. What is difficult about school for your child?

   _____

   _____

6. What are your child's strengths or areas of expertise? What is he or she really, really good at?

   _____

   _____

Sincerely,

Tools 12 and 13: Structured Interviews

Keeping the Bright Turned On!

❏ **Who Am I?:** Have students pick a way to introduce themselves to the class. Their product/presentation should reflect their strengths and interests. Having the opportunity to share is an important component so that peers begin to recognize each other's strengths.

❏ **My Hero:** Have students pick a person they admire who has overcome an obstacle. It can be someone famous or someone that they know personally. Have them create a way to introduce this person to the class, explaining why they admire him or her. For example, they could write a poem or song, make a collage, or act out the obstacle the hero overcame.

❏ **See Me, Hear Me—This Is Me:** Make an outline of the student's body with lines coming from various parts: with my hands I can; with my feet I can; with my thoughts I can; with my eyes I can (this shows students that their strengths come from all parts of the body).

❏ **Jar Joys:** Have strips of paper on which the student writes down accomplishments, skills acquired, and new talents and strengths discovered. Have the student place them in the jar. Parents and/or teachers have a separate jar and do the same. From time to time they share/compare. (Idea shared by Joan Ridge and Amy Wish, mentors from the WINGS Mentor Program, Montgomery County Public Schools, Montgomery County, MD.)

chapter 2

How Do I Find These Kids?

He is educated who knows how to find out what he doesn't know.
—George Simmel

Guiding Questions

❑ What are obstacles to the appropriate identification of these students?

❑ What are best practices for identification of these students? What are the formal/informal tools used to identify them?

❑ What are ways I can recognize and free potential strengths within my students? How do I unmask their gifts?

❑ What are ways I can recognize their learning difficulties? How do I unmask their learning problems?

Word Sparks

✓ identification
✓ masking
✓ obstacles
✓ data sources
✓ criteria
✓ performance
✓ perfectionism
✓ multiple intelligences

✓ stumbling blocks
✓ ORR
✓ writing
✓ organization
✓ reading
✓ memory
✓ emotional overexcitability
✓ social/emotional

Chapter Overview

IN the previous chapter, you met Sarah, Jeremy, and Darryl and learned about the characteristics of bright students with learning difficulties. Now we will examine various sources of data that will help you to recognize previously unidentified students in your classroom. Proper identification of these students requires careful analysis of multiple sources of information about the students' strengths and needs to form a complete picture of the students. Although we know there are formal processes in most school districts for identifying students as gifted and for determining eligibility for an IEP or 504 Plan, this book does not focus on helping you navigate those processes. Rather, the focus is on helping you find ways to uncover a student's amazing strengths and surprising difficulties so that you can begin to unleash his potential and improve his weaker areas. This process may lead to or inform formal identification of a student as gifted or as having a disability, but it is not the primary intention of this book to label students.

Obstacles to Appropriate Identification

First, let's discuss what makes these students so hard to find. It is commonly understood that these students (also called twice-exceptional students) do exist. The prevalence is unknown because no federal agency gathers data for this population, but estimates suggest there are approximately 360,000 twice-exceptional students in U.S. schools (National Association for Gifted Children, 2008). Therefore, it is fairly reasonable to assume that every school has bright students with learning difficulties and, if you have been teaching for a while, that you have taught these special students before, whether you knew it or not. Morrison and Rizza (2007) suggested that identification of these students is problematic and the main obstacle is a lack of teacher understanding of the characteristics of this population. Simply put, many educators do not know what to look for and do not recognize these students when they see them.

Another factor impacting the appropriate identification of these students is a belief held by some educators that a gifted student cannot have a disability. The identification procedures guided by federal and state regulations are thus largely focused on the needs of students who are failing and are years below grade level. This type of approach to an identification model is problematic for bright students with learning problems because it presupposes that a student must be failing before he would be considered for evaluation or identification as a student with a disability. These methods assume that the definition for failure for a gifted child is the same as the definition for children of average or below-average cognitive ability. Within this framework, average achievement scores are ignored. This is a huge mistake, because average performance can signify a failure to thrive in gifted students. Proper identification of bright students with learning difficulties requires an appreciation for potential versus actual achievement. Current models for identification of students with a disability do not always properly take into account student potential (Morrison & Rizza, 2007).

An additional factor that often precludes the appropriate identification of these students involves the concept of "masking" (Brody & Mills, 1997). Bright students with learning difficulties mask themselves in different ways:

1. *Those whose gifts mask their learning problems.* These students are often perceived to be bright but unmotivated or lazy. This group of students is most likely to be identified by schools as gifted but too often the learning problems are not recognized. Thus, they do not receive services to address their difficulties.
2. *Those whose learning problems mask their gifts.* These students are often perceived to be slow, and their disability is formally identified. Their strengths and abilities are not recognized; thus, they do not receive services to address their gifts.
3. *Those whose gifts and learning problems mask one another.* These students are often perceived to be simply average. These students are most at risk because they do not receive services for their difficulties or for their gifts.

Identification of bright students with learning difficulties is further compounded when we consider those from traditionally underserved populations. African American and Hispanic students, students from low-socioeconomic groups, English language learners, and girls are all commonly underrepresented within the twice-exceptional population. Despite the fact that giftedness crosses all racial, gender, and economic lines, these populations are underrepresented in most gifted programs. Teachers do not always equitably recognize and nurture the indicators of gifted ability within students from different groups. This chapter will empower you to recognize all students who are bright and have learning difficulties so that they can receive both the challenges and support that they need to be successful. Being aware of the inequities and knowing the characteristics of smart kids with learning difficulties are the first steps in finding these students.

Best Practices for Identification

Although these students are hard to find, the task is not impossible! Consideration of the following best practices for identification of a bright student with learning difficulties is recommended:

✓ collect and review multiple and varied sources of data to establish a pattern of strengths and weaknesses;

✓ use multiple criteria that examine the whole profile from different perspectives, including verbal, nonverbal, and creativity measures;

✓ include information from all stakeholders: teachers, parents, the student, and other school staff;

✓ use a nontraditional view of identification that acknowledges the possibility that a student can be gifted and have learning difficulties;

✓ focus on the student as an individual in order to identify significant and meaningful differences between strengths and weaknesses;

✓ compare the student's performance to that of her gifted peers or to her own ability rather than to age- or grade-level expectations;

✓ disregard arbitrary performance benchmarks or cut-scores (low or high) that may be used to determine appropriate services; and

✓ include at least one person who is well-versed in the needs and characteristics of these students on the identification team

Remember, when reviewing data, trust a high score. There are many reasons why a child will underperform, but only one reason why a child performs well.

Data Sources

There are many sources of information that will reveal the signature "scattered profile" that is the red flag of a possible bright student with learning problems.

✓ Classroom performance data (e.g., report cards, anecdotal teacher records, unit assessments, quizzes, writing samples, work products from a variety of content areas) will often show that the student does very well on some tasks and very poorly on others.

✓ Formal, standardized tests (e.g., IQ tests, nonverbal measures, creativity assessments, achievement tests, district- and statewide assessments) often reveal broad areas of strengths and weaknesses. However, it is important to realize that these students often perform very well on standardized assessments, so teams should not rely solely on this source of data to rule out a learning problem.

✓ Informal assessments (e.g., reading inventories, running records, writing samples) are critical, as they help the team drill down to analyze the student's strengths and weaknesses within a given area.

✓ Structured observations of the student (during areas of strength as well as tasks where the student is suspected to have a learning problem) reveal how the student functions in the classroom on typical assignments and tasks. Observations often show that they have areas of academic strength yet seem unable to perform at expected levels on a day-to-day basis without intensive support.

✓ Interviews with the student, her parents, and other significant adults reveal other perspectives. These students often act differently at school than they do at home or in the community, so this information should be included. Students with learning difficulties often feel as though they are different and have low self-esteem, so targeted questions about school can reveal this piece of the puzzle.

✓ Checklists, surveys, and rating scales (e.g., ADHD or Asperger's rating scales, Renzulli-Hartman gifted behavior rating scale, Multiple Intelligences surveys) can help you see things you might not otherwise have noticed by focusing your attention on patterns of behavior and performance. These often reveal that the student possesses many typical characteristics of a gifted student and of a student with a specific disability.

✓ Student activities (e.g., learning style surveys, interest inventories, projects, performance tasks) can be designed to generate information about the student's strengths that would not be revealed within a traditional classroom. Often the student will "light up" or "spark" and demonstrate a creative or well-reasoned response to a task or problem. Many of the tools in this chapter fall into this category and will help you ignite that spark.

These are just some of the data sources that can be used to gather and analyze information about your students as you seek to understand their unique learner profiles. Some may be at your disposal while others are not. The important thing is to seek out all available data and to supplement that information with other sources that are within your power to administer or collect.

Social/Emotional Considerations Related to Identification

As previously discussed, these students often mask their gifts and difficulties, flying under the radar and obscuring early identification and intervention. Over time, the frustration and anxiety related to their school stress intensifies and their negative feelings and emotions often begin to manifest. This might look like sadness and withdrawal or it might look like anger and opposition. The behavior can be passive or quite aggressive. Often it is the emerging behaviors that trigger concerns from the school team. In these situations, it is essential to consider whether the behavior is a result of the academic struggles or the cause of them. Analysis of the function of the behaviors will often reveal that they occur only during certain academic tasks (reading or writing), in certain settings (at school but not at home or vice versa), or that they have developed over time (intensifying during school years as academic expectations increase). The team must not rule out learning issues when they see emerging behavior problems in gifted underachieving students. In fact, this is a critical red flag that a learning issue may exist and should trigger problem-solving discussions for these students, which might lead to a formal evaluation process.

Perfectionism and emotional overexcitability also have relevance for identification of this population. In Chapter 1, we discussed how these two traits could prevent teachers from identifying bright kids for the special programming they will need. Perfectionism can keep them from completing classwork and homework that does not live up to their expectations, thereby preventing the teacher from having the opportunity to assess their learning needs. Emotional overexcitability may result in behaviors that interfere with group learning and self-directed learning. Students may appear socially inappropriate, disinterested, or confused. Therefore the teacher's knowledge and understanding of these traits is critical to obtaining accurate information and the ability to advocate in school meetings when identifying these young people for the services and programming they will need.

Student Profiles

Sarah

Sarah's parents always knew that she was smart. She began talking at a very young age, using complex grammar and vocabulary way beyond her years. On the playground she would often play alone, creating fantastical worlds and stories using ordinary objects. Yet at the same time, Sarah's parents described her early on as a "difficult child." They would give her simple directions (e.g., "Make your bed") that she could not follow, she often (seemingly innocently) broke rules that they attempted to impose, and she never seemed to pick up on routines. They saw her younger siblings as much more independent and focused and wondered what was wrong with Sarah.

Sarah's preschool, kindergarten, and first-grade teachers also clearly saw her brilliance and her difficulty with following directions, rules, and routines. However, they felt that Sarah could easily meet the expectations set before her if she desired to. In fact, during art activities, Sarah was so extremely focused that it was difficult to get her to stop working on her masterpieces. They determined that the issues were behavioral and they set up a system of clear rewards and consequences for her. Sadly, Sarah did not respond favorably to this behavior system despite the fact that she was initially enthusiastic about earning the stickers. She seemed unable to do what was being asked of her at times, while she sailed easily through complex activities. Her reading level was advanced and her spelling was quite good. Despite the fact that her academic skills were developing appropriately (and in many cases, at an advanced pace), her frustration grew over these 2 years, and by the end of first grade, Sarah was avoiding tasks and passively ignoring her teacher's directions. Sarah's parents asked the teachers to provide more assistance with her work, but they felt strongly that this would only enable her and make her more dependent on the adults. They had concluded that Sarah was unmotivated, and she would perform up to her ability when she wanted to. There was nothing more they felt they could do.

Sarah entered second grade a reluctant learner. But Mrs. Smith was an experienced teacher who had taught many smart kids with learning problems, and she suspected early on that Sarah was incredibly intelligent, but that she had attention problems that were interfering with her success. Although she wasn't hyperactive, she was terribly inattentive and impulsive and seemed to lack necessary executive functioning skills. Mrs. Smith talked with Sarah's parents and collaborated with the grade-level team to develop and document supports for Sarah while simultaneously providing challenging instruction that stimulated and engaged Sarah. Recognizing Sarah's significant pattern of strengths and weaknesses, she ultimately suggested to Sarah's parents that they might want to bring the attention concerns to their pediatrician, who diagnosed Sarah with ADHD-Inattentive Type. Armed with this knowledge, Sarah's team eventually identified Sarah as a student with a disability and developed an IEP for her that formally outlined her supports and accommodations.

Jeremy

Given the nature and visibility of Jeremy's social difficulties, his parents took him to their pediatrician and had him privately evaluated when he was 5 years old. He was diagnosed at that time with Asperger's syndrome and has received some support for his disability ever since. His IEP was developed right away when he entered the school system. However, it took some time before the school realized just how bright Jeremy was and responded. His teachers realized that he was bored in math, he could read anything they put in front of him, and he already knew everything they were teaching in social studies and science, but he had trouble with writing. Because he was socially immature, they never thought about putting him in advanced groups or giving him accelerated work; they were focused on supporting his social and behavioral needs. Then, the school conducted their GT identification process for all students and Jeremy scored off the charts on the verbal reasoning portions of the assessments. They checked into his records and realized his IQ scores on those tests supported the fact that he had amazing verbal ability. They reviewed his academic data and realized that Jeremy was, in fact, a gifted student with Asperger's and that they needed to focus on challenging Jeremy as well as supporting him.

Darryl

"What's wrong with being average?" Darryl's first- and second-grade teachers would ask when his parents expressed concern about his delayed reading and writing ability and his boredom and frustration at school. "He's making progress," they would say. "He's just fine! Students develop at different rates and he'll catch up. He's a happy kid, there's nothing wrong." But he didn't catch up, and by third grade, Darryl didn't seem so happy anymore. His third-grade teacher became very concerned when she realized that not only was he still behind his peers in reading decoding and fluency, but the gap had actually widened since first grade. His parents told her he had started saying he was stupid and didn't want to go to school. She worked with the grade-level team and the counselor to develop and document interventions for Darryl. He made slight progress, but it just wasn't clicking. The counselor worked with him and found that his self-esteem was suffering. He began to shut down and withdraw during reading lessons. By the end of the second quarter, the team felt they had enough data to refer Darryl for evaluation. The testing confirmed that Darryl was 2 years below grade level in written expression, basic reading skills, and reading fluency. His math calculation skills were weak, but his mathematical reasoning was superior. To his first- and second-grade teachers' surprise, Darryl was anything but average. His cognitive ability (both verbal and visual reasoning) was at the 98th percentile. The team determined that Darryl was GT/LD and eligible for special education services.

Conclusion

This chapter will empower you to recognize all students who are bright and have learning difficulties so that they can receive both the challenge and support that they need to be successful. Being aware of the inequities and knowing the characteristics of smart kids with learning difficulties are the first steps in finding these students. Appropriate identification is only the beginning of the journey for kids like Sarah, Jeremy, and Darryl, but it is a critical first step. The identification can be formal (IEP or 504 Plan) or informal, but the key is recognizing the student's strengths and weaknesses.

The tools in this chapter will empower you to provide your students with many opportunities to show you their strengths and will give you ways to collect information on their weaknesses as well. These tools will support your development of a stronger understanding of the characteristics of bright kids with learning difficulties and increase your ability to spot them in your classroom. This knowledge will be the key to moving forward in future chapters as we explore ways to ensure the success of your students.

Tool 14:
Data Capture Sheet

When trying to recognize gifted students with learning difficulties, the goal is to see beyond the masks of disability, behavior, culture, poverty, and language to reveal the student's true strengths and weaknesses.

Tips

✓ *Tool 14: Data Capture Sheet.* Use this capture sheet as you review all available data regarding a student that you suspect may be a bright student with learning differences. Where do you find all of this information? Much of it can be found in the student's school records, so start there. Then, talk to other teachers and specialists in your school.

Tool 14: Data Capture Sheet

Tool 14: Data Capture Sheet

Individual Assessment Data
Description of data source: Individually administered achievement tests, aptitude/ability tests (IQ), rating scales
Such as: Woodcock-Johnson III Normative Update (WJ III), Weschler Intelligence Scale for Children (WISC-IV), Conners Rating Scales–Revised, Behavior Rating Inventory of Executive Function (BRIEF), Behavior Assessment System for Children, Second Edition (BASC-2), Gilliam Asperger's Disorder Scale (GADS)
Data:

Strengths revealed:	Weaknesses revealed:

District and Statewide Assessments
Description of data source: Assessments administered to all children in the school
Such as: Maryland School Assessment (MSA), California Achievement Tests (CAT), Raven's Progressive Matrices (Coloured, Standard, Advanced), InView Cognitive Abilities Test, Measures of Academic Progress in Reading (MAP-R)
Data:

Strengths revealed:	Weaknesses revealed:

Tool 14: Data Capture Sheet

Tool 14: Data Capture Sheet

Classroom Performance Data
Description of data source: Curriculum assessments, running records, informal reading inventories, writing samples, products
Such as: math tests, science quizzes, scored writing assignments, Basic Reading Inventory
Data:

Strengths revealed:	Weaknesses revealed:

Informal Data
Description of data source: Information from parents, teachers, and the student
Such as: interviews, questionnaires, observations, anecdotal records, checklists
Data:

Strengths revealed:	Weaknesses revealed:

Tools 15 and 16:
Many Ways to Be Smart!

In 1983, Howard Gardner, a professor at Harvard University, introduced his theory of multiple intelligences (MI) in his book *Frames of Mind: The Theory of Multiple Intelligences*. His theory provided us with new ways to look at intelligence and observe, understand, and teach children. Using MI will help students understand their strengths, interests, and talents while at the same time offering them alternative avenues to share what they know.

Tips

- ✓ *Tool 15: Many Ways to Be Smart Chart.* Review the information on the chart to familiarize yourself with the eight intelligences that Gardner has identified. Carefully observe your students to determine their MI strengths and preferences. Record student names and any notes in the righthand column.
- ✓ *Tool 16: Parent Partnership Piece: Many Ways to Be Smart Chart.* Send a copy of the chart from Tool 15 home with the letter.

Tool 15: Many Ways to Be Smart Chart

Way of Learning	Things They May Enjoy	Instructional Implications	Observations/Notes
Verbal/Linguistic • thinks in words • good speaker • has highly receptive and/or expressive developed vocabulary	• listening to stories • talking • word games • writing	*Emphasize:* read-alouds, discussions, high-level questioning, debates, shared inquiry, think-pair-share *Products:* oral presentations, dictated written responses, poetry, letters, crosswords, newspapers, journals, interviews	Future public speakers and historians:
Visual/Spatial • tends to think in pictures • uses mental images to retain information • learns and uses diagrams, maps, charts, pictures, videos, etc.	• designing • drawing/doodling • building • sorting • puzzles • watching videos • art	*Emphasize:* hands-on learning, manipulatives, visuals, visual imagery *Products:* dioramas, posters, collages, drawings, diagrams, animation/cartoons/comic strips, book jackets, videos/movies	Future artists and graphic designers:

Way of Learning	Things They May Enjoy	Instructional Implications	Observations/Notes
Logical/Mathematical • uses reason, logic, and numbers • thinks conceptually in logical and numerical patterns • likes to experiment	• experiments • questioning • science and math • solving challenging problems	*Emphasize:* open-ended tasks and questions, problem-based learning, deductive reasoning, charts and statistics *Products:* charts, graphs, fact files, inventions, observation logs, experiments	Future scientists and mathematicians:
Bodily/Kinesthetic • controls body movements and handles objects skillfully • good hand-eye coordination • learns through interacting with space around him	• running • dancing • jumping • building • sports	*Emphasize:* movement, dramatic interpretation, role-play, dance, hands-on learning, manipulatives *Products:* costumes, dance, demonstrations, experiments, operas, plays, physical games, mime, tableaux vivants (living pictures), visual art, simulations	Future dancers and athletes:

Tools 15 and 16: Many Ways to Be Smart!

Tools 15 and 16: Many Ways to Be Smart!

Way of Learning	Things They May Enjoy	Instructional Implications	Observations/Notes
Musical/ Rhythmic • appreciates music • produces music • thinks in sounds, rhythms, and patterns	• singing • whistling • humming • listening to music • tapping feet	*Emphasize:* sing-alongs, songs for learning, music related to concepts and topics, rhythms and patterns in the curriculum *Products:* songs, choreography, musical interpretations, song lists, musicals	Future musicians and songwriters:
Interpersonal • relates to others • understands others • sees things from other perspectives	• group work • socializing • leading/ following • sharing and listening to opinions	*Emphasize:* cooperative grouping, group problem solving, group games, student-to-student dialogue *Products:* open-ended group products, debates, collaborative writing tasks, expert groups, jigsaws	Future politicians and teachers:

Way of Learning	Things They May Enjoy	Instructional Implications	Observations/Notes
Intrapersonal • uses self-reflection • aware of own state of being • understands own feelings, relationships with others, and her own strengths and needs	• being alone • working and playing alone • setting personal goals • reflecting on opinions • connecting to personal experiences	*Emphasize:* time for individual reflection, processing, and sharing; text-to-self connections; self-paced projects; task choices *Products:* journals, diaries, art for self-expression, blogs, personal web page	Future authors and artists:
Naturalist • understands his environment • applies science to own life • recognizes connection to nature	• being in nature • animals • environmental issues • gardening	*Emphasize:* interaction with nature, natural phenomena, environmental context, text/self-to-world connections, current events, scientific principles *Products:* nature walks, natural artifacts	Future veterinarians and global ecologists:

Note. Adapted from Armstrong (2000).

Tools 15 and 16: Many Ways to Be Smart!

Tool 16: Parent Partnership Piece
Many Ways to Be Smart Chart

Dear Parent,

In class, we have been discussing the following questions: What kind of learner am I? What are my strengths? What are my preferences?

In 1983, Howard Gardner, a professor at Harvard University, described intelligence as multifaceted and introduced his theory of multiple intelligences (MI), which provides us with new ways to look at intelligence, as well as a new way to observe, understand, and teach children. Using MI will allow students to learn in many ways and will help them understand their strengths, interests, and talents, while at the same time offering them alternative avenues to share what they know. Attached is a chart of the eight different intelligences and brief descriptions of what you might see at home with your child. Remember that your child possesses all eight intelligences in different degrees, even though he or she may prefer one or two. Gardner's work in the multiple intelligences can help you uncover gifts that may be hidden.

Talk with your child about his or her strengths, interests, and talents and how he or she lets people know what he or she knows. On the attached chart, circle the intelligences that are evident to you when you are observing your child. Record observations that support the use of the specific multiple intelligence in the righthand column. Share this information with me.

Sincerely,

Tool 17:
Task Masters

Teachers should not just know their students' strengths, but also should teach students about the different types of intelligences. This self-awareness makes them able to help teachers develop alternative assignments that allow them to show what they know through their strengths.

Tips

✓ *Tool 17: Student Tool: Task Masters.* In this activity, students will learn about the different intelligences. Present the students with a topic based on your curriculum (e.g., fractions, the Civil War, cell structures) and have them choose one of the tasks to show what they know about the topic.

- Have students move to identified areas based on their task selections. (Little do they know, they have chosen an MI preference!) Tell them that they have 10–20 minutes to complete the task and they may work alone or with partners/groups.

- Have each student/group present the work/task. Teach the class about the eight intelligences and help them determine which intelligence each group used. Students will begin to recognize the strengths of their peers and themselves—perhaps strengths that they may not have realized before.

- Have students think of people they know who are good in the different intelligences. Have them think of what their own preferences/strengths may be. Post the names of the different intelligences around the room for students to reference.

Tool 17: Task Masters

Tool 17: Student Tool
Task Masters

Directions: Select a task that appeals to you!

Topic: _____

Write a poem that shows what you know about the topic.	Create a top 10 list that shows what you know about the topic.	Create a drawing or other visual representation that shows what you know about the topic.	Create a short skit or dance that shows what you know about the topic.
Write a song or rap that shows what you know about the topic.	As a group, determine a good way to show what you know about the topic.	Write yourself a letter reflecting upon what you've learned about the topic and its importance to you.	Develop a product that shows how the topic relates to the natural world (the environment and the creatures that live in it).

Tools 18 and 19:
Multiple Intelligences
Card Activities

When students have the opportunity to pick their own projects to show what they know about a subject, they will naturally draw on their strengths. Giving them choices based on MI will allow you to capitalize upon their strengths and abilities. Once you know the multiple intelligences of your students, you can use the information as a basis for determining teams for group projects. Each team could have strengths in the different intelligences, or you could group students with similar strengths together.

Tips

✓ *Tool 18: Student Tool: Project Picks.* Introduce the multiple intelligences to the class and place the tool on the board or overhead. Have the students come up with examples of types of projects that someone with that intelligence might enjoy. Record their project ideas under the intelligence.

✓ *Tool 19: MI Card Sort.* Divide the class into small groups. Give each group a set of the Project Picks cards and an envelope with the MI Card Sort pieces. Instruct the students to read each of the pieces and to classify the projects into MI categories by matching the piece to the appropriate Project Pick card. For example, someone with spatial intelligence could enjoy painting a picture or performing a dance. After students have worked in small groups, have each group share how it classified the projects. If there are disagreements as to in which intelligence category a project belongs, discuss the reasoning for the students' classification. Are there projects/skills that may fall into more than one intelligence/strength category? Next, give students a copy of the MI Card Sort pieces page (or use Tool 9) and have them circle ones that are appealing to them. Ask them to tell you what this says about their multiple intelligences.

✓ Create a community of learners! Explain to the class that when you draw on other people's strengths to get work done, you become a community of learners. Not everyone is good at everything. Have the students decide which intelligences are their strongest. List the names of the students under each of the intelligences. Keep the list posted somewhere in the classroom. Explain how people can rely on each other to help them in areas in which they may struggle. Provide opportunities in assignments for students to team up, combining the strengths of their peers to complete work.

Tools 18 and 19: Multiple Intelligences Card Activities

Tool 18: Student Tool
Project Picks

Directions: Identify projects that would tap into each strength/intelligence area.

Verbal/Linguistic	Logical/Mathematical
Visual/Spatial	Musical
Naturalist	Bodily-Kinesthetic
Interpersonal	Intrapersonal

Tools 18 and 19: Multiple Intelligences Card Activities

Tool 19: MI Card Sort

Debate	Speech	Story	Poem
Cartoon	PowerPoint	Sculpture	Diary Entry
Chart	Diagram	Graph	Survey
Song	Musical Skit	Write a Jingle	Poster
Artifact Collection	Experiment	Observation Log	Brochure
Script for Skit	Dance	Mime/Tableau	Puppet Show
Journal	Photo Essay	Painting	Newspaper/Report
Interview	Role-Play	Web Page	Video/Movie

Tools 18 and 19: Multiple Intelligences Card Activities

Tools 20–24: Project Shine!

Projects provide the perfect arena for students to approach tasks, learn information, and demonstrate understanding through their areas of strength. Through projects, students become actively engaged in their learning. In schools, there is strong emphasis placed on the verbal/linguistic and logical/mathematical intelligences, both in teaching and assessing. Unfortunately, those students who do not shine in those areas often are seen as not having any gifts (Gardner, 1993). Projects are a way for students to reveal their gifts and shine!

Tips

✓ *Tool 20: Student Tool: Project Planning Chart.* Use this tool to help students break down their project into manageable chunks and set short-term goals.

✓ *Tool 21: Project Evaluation.* Use when the project is completed to reflect about what it has taught you about the student through the process.

✓ *Tools 22 and 23: Student Tool: Project Self-Reflection* and *Student Tool: Using My Strengths.* Students should be given the opportunity to evaluate their own work and reflect on what they have learned. Use the following tools, develop one of your own, or even better, develop a self-evaluation tool with the students.

✓ *Tool 24: Student Interview—Reflection on Strengths.* As a component of your evaluation of student projects, use the interview questions to gain information on how a specific student perceived his strengths and those of his peers.

Tool 20: Student Tool
Project Planning Chart

Student Name: _____

Class: _____

Project Title: _____

Due Date: _____

For a long-term or multistep project, break down the task into its component parts. Set mini-deadlines for each component. Get feedback from your teacher at each mini-deadline.

❑   Step 1: _____   Date due: _____

❑   Step 2: _____   Date due: _____

❑   Step 3: _____   Date due: _____

❑   Step 4: _____   Date due: _____

❑   Step 5: _____   Date due: _____

❑   Step 6: _____   Date due: _____

❑   Step 7: _____   Date due: _____

❑   Step 8: _____   Date due: _____

❑   Step 9: _____   Date due: _____

❑   Step 10: _____   Date due: _____

Notes:

Tool 21: Project Evaluation

Student Name: _____

Project Title: _____

Objective (What was the student expected to learn?): _____

_____

1. To what degree does the project reflect mastery of the facts, concepts, or skills?

   _____

   _____

   _____

   _____

2. What does the project reveal about the student's strengths, interests, learning style, and multiple intelligences?

   _____

   _____

   _____

   _____

3. To what degree does the project show risk taking and/or perseverance?

   _____

   _____

   _____

   _____

Tools 20–24: Project Shine!

Tool 22: Student Tool
Project Self-Reflection

Directions: Complete the following questions on the computer, with another classmate, or with the teacher. Be prepared to discuss them.

Name of Project: _____

1. What was the goal of your project?

    _____

    _____

    _____

    _____

2. How well do you feel that you achieved your goal?

    _____

    _____

    _____

    _____

3. Which of the multiple intelligences did you use to complete the project?

    _____

    _____

    _____

    _____

4. Did you discover any new strengths or interests that you had while completing the project?

    _____

    _____

    _____

    _____

Tool 23: Student Tool
Using My Strengths

Directions: Based on your project, think about each category listed below and decide to what degree you accomplished the goal. Be honest with yourself!

Project Title: _____

	Planning	Design	Creativity	Effort	Achieved goal	Other area _____
Awesome achievement						
Better than most						
Pretty good						
Getting there						
Room for improvement						

Tools 20–24: Project Shine!

Tool 24: Student Interview— Reflection on Strengths

Directions: Set up a time to meet with your students individually to discuss the following questions:

1. Thinking about what you have learned about multiple intelligences, which of the multiple intelligences do you consider to be your strengths?

   _____

   _____

2. How did your project allow you to utilize your MI strengths?

   _____

   _____

3. When working with a partner, it is ideal if you are able to draw on each other's strengths. If you could seek out a classmate to help you with a class project, which type of intelligence would he or she exhibit?

   _____

   _____

4. What have you learned over the past few weeks about yourself and the type of learner you are?

   _____

   _____

5. If you could practice and become good in one of the multiple intelligences, which would you choose?

   _____

   _____

Tools 20–24: Project Shine!

Tools 25–29: Applying Observe and Reflect and Respond (ORR)

Children give us clues that help us recognize their potential. Teachers can help their students find the power within themselves by using the process we call Observe and Reflect and Respond (ORR; see Barnes-Robinson, Jeweler, & Ricci, 2004, 2009, and Ricci, Barnes-Robinson, & Jeweler, 2006 for more information). The ORR process can provide a way to focus in on any given area where you need to learn more about a child. You can use it to learn about the student's strengths using multiple intelligences or to learn more about the student's academic or social/emotional needs. Column 1 describes a specific observable behavior, Column 2 lists questions that you can ask yourself during reflection, and Column 3 offers possible actions that may nurture this strength. The charts are not all-inclusive lists, but rather examples designed to stimulate your own thinking.

Tips

✓ *Tool 25: Visual Spatial ORR.* As we make every effort to tap into the strengths, interests, and expertise of our students while they work and play in the world around them, the ORR process can facilitate getting to know our visual-spatial learners better. These students live in a world that revolves around the spoken word; therefore we must learn to help them meet the challenges they face in this environment. By focusing on what gifts the visual-spatial learners bring to the table, we can identify and nurture their strengths while supporting any learning difficulties.

✓ *Tool 26: Academic ORR.* This chart illustrates how the model can be used when analyzing a student in the academic areas.

✓ *Tools 27 and 28: Perfectionism ORR* and *Emotional Overexcitability ORR.* Some students come to us with existing social/emotional difficulties for whatever reason. Many bright kids with learning difficulties develop social/emotional problems as a result of unidentified and unaddressed learning problems. These behaviors can be our first clues that something is just not right.

✓ *Tool 29: ORR Template.* This blank template can be used to observe, reflect, and respond to an individual student in any area (e.g., cognitive, multiple intelligences, academic).

Tool 25: Visual Spatial ORR

Observe	Reflect	Respond
Projects are often constructions, structures, and visual and spatial presentations.	■ Does my student prefer building to books? ■ How are the structures unique? ■ How can I support her interest and ability?	■ Make building and art materials available in the classroom. ■ Allow alternative products for assignments. ■ Showcase her creations in the classroom. ■ Make sure she is familiar with PowerPoint, Kidspiration, and other platforms for expressing information visually.
Likes to spend time making things, doing arts and crafts, and attending art class.	■ How do I validate her ability? ■ What kinds of materials does she choose to work with? ■ Where do her ideas come from? ■ How can I promote her strengths and interest? ■ How can I infuse this interest into my instruction?	■ Save lots of "stuff" for her to find new uses for (e.g., paper towel rolls, empty tape dispensers, PVC pipe). ■ Go to the library for "what makes it work" illustrated books. ■ Create an exhibit of her creations. ■ Arrange for a visit to museums and galleries. ■ Allow her to show mastery of her learning through art.
Can accomplish complex tasks with many steps, but sometimes can find simple tasks challenging.	■ How does she approach or begin a task? ■ Can she identify the process used to accomplish a complex task with many steps? ■ Does she understand how the steps build on one another? ■ How can I help her with tasks that are challenging?	■ Talk to her about how she thinks/sees when doing complex tasks. ■ Identify simple steps within complex or difficult tasks. ■ Ask questions like, "What did you do first? What did you do next?" ■ Teach her to formulate questions to ask herself.

Observe	Reflect	Respond
Looks at pictures rather than words when working on assignments.	<ul><li>Can I help her express herself in words?</li><li>How can I capitalize on how she conceptualizes tasks?</li></ul>	<ul><li>Provide diagrams.</li><li>Offer project alternatives where she can use pictures to show what she knows.</li></ul>
Can remember how to get somewhere after only going there once (e.g., layout of school, places in the community).	<ul><li>How does she know where to go?</li><li>Does she recognize familiar landmarks?</li><li>How can she use this strength in other situations?</li></ul>	<ul><li>Ask her to articulate what she uses to remember directions (e.g., colors, patterns).</li><li>Help her recognize this strength and its usefulness in other situations.</li></ul>
Has great creativity and imagination demonstrated in drawing, building, make-believe play, and responses to questions. Displays strengths in original ideas, elaboration of thought, generation of ideas (fluency), and ideas in multiple categories (flexibility).	<ul><li>How can I encourage her creativity and imagination?</li><li>How can I infuse nurturing of creativity into my everyday instruction?</li></ul>	<ul><li>Plan lessons that raise creativity consciousness in my classroom.</li><li>Choose materials for her that stimulate and require imagination.</li><li>Offer her opportunities in class to express her creativity and imagination.</li><li>Reinforce her by saying, "Great idea!" or "You have a super imagination!" or "Wow, where do your great ideas come from?"</li></ul>

Tools 25–29: Applying Observe and Reflect and Respond (ORR)

Tool 26: Academic ORR

Observe	Reflect	Respond
Reads slowly and has weak decoding skills, thus he does not comprehend text read independently.	▪ Has the student received systematic instruction in phonemic awareness and phonics? ▪ Is he making progress?	▪ Provide systematic/decoding reading instruction and collect progress data frequently.
Listens raptly during read-alouds and participates orally in discussions about text, making inferences and connections easily.	▪ Is the student's listening comprehension ability significantly stronger than his basic reading ability?	▪ Include the student in high-level reading groups with appropriate supports (e.g., recorded books, read-alouds).
Writes with nonphonetic spelling. Written vocabulary use does not match with oral vocabulary sophistication.	▪ Does the student lack phonemic awareness and sound-symbol association required for phonetic spelling?	▪ Provide systematic decoding/encoding instruction.
Writes minimally with little elaboration, support, or detail despite ability to share orally at length and in great detail.	▪ Does the student have executive functioning or organizational challenges that are interfering with his ability to express his ideas in writing?	▪ Provide instruction in strategies for developing and organizing ideas prior to writing (e.g., graphic organizers, outlines, lists). ▪ Take dictation or provide verbal preconference.
Makes frequent errors in math calculation and lacks automatic recall of basic math facts despite having advanced math-reasoning ability.	▪ Does the student's difficulty interfere with his ability to solve higher level math problems? ▪ Does the student have the number sense but lack the memory for the facts?	▪ Provide a calculator or reference sheet to support calculations (e.g., multiplication table) during math problem-solving tasks.

Observe	Reflect	Respond
Great in science but has difficulty completing the steps of experiments.	▪ Does the student have difficulty following multistep directions?	▪ Partner with a student with strong organizational skills. ▪ Provide written checklists.
Great ideas for a project but lacks follow-through and doesn't get it done.	▪ Does the student have difficulty planning and executing long-term tasks?	▪ Break down the task into smaller parts. ▪ Frequently check the student's progress on the project.

Tools 25–29: Applying Observe and Reflect and Respond (ORR)

Tool 27: Perfectionism ORR

Observe	Reflect	Respond
Sets goals appropriate to potential but other things, such as motor skills and peer relationships, may frustrate her if they get in the way of her goal. Sets lofty goals that are never achieved.	▪ Is the student unable to live up to her own (or others') expectations? ▪ Are there organizational problems that are interfering with her ability to plan or to follow through with plans? ▪ Are there skill deficits (e.g., reading, writing) that limit the student's performance?	▪ Together, set realistic goals. ▪ Help the student conduct a task analysis and develop a written checklist/timeline for her to follow. ▪ Check progress frequently.
Is not always satisfied with her performance or herself (e.g., destroys papers, makes negative comments about work samples, avoids work, puts self down, says "I'm stupid").	▪ Why is my student dissatisfied? ▪ What kinds of things cause the most difficulty for her? ▪ What school expectations are contributing to this issue? ▪ Are the student's expectations too high or is the performance poor? ▪ Could this be due to possible learning difficulties?	▪ Adjust my own behavior. ▪ With her, set more realistic expectations. ▪ Help her recognize and feel good about accomplishing her personal best. ▪ Help her realistically evaluate her tasks at school. ▪ Give the student specific positive feedback and provide support so that she is able to produce a quality product she can be proud of.

Tool 28: Emotional Overexcitability ORR

Observe	Reflect	Respond
Experiences intense emotional reactions to people, ideas, and things.	▪ Under what circumstances or in what subjects does this behavior occur? ▪ Are there patterns that emerge that speak to a learning problem?	▪ Be accepting of intense feelings and help the student work through the problem. ▪ Help him recognize the triggers or warning signs when he becomes upset. ▪ Work with him to find coping mechanisms. ▪ Communicate with the counselor for additional support. ▪ Document and support the learning challenges that are causing frustration.
May appear overly sensitive.	▪ In what situations does this occur most frequently? ▪ Are there specific things that trigger this behavior? ▪ Does it happen a lot? ▪ Does it manifest in the same way (e.g., cry, shut down, retreat, outburst)?	▪ Brainstorm coping strategies with him when in these situations. ▪ Role-play some difficult situations and implement coping strategies at home and at school after discussions with school counselor and parents.
Blames others, objects, and events when things go wrong.	▪ Why doesn't my student take some responsibility when things go wrong? ▪ Is there a pattern to this behavior? ▪ Are there some instances when he does take responsibility?	▪ When a task is difficult, work with him to break it down into doable steps. ▪ Discuss what happens when things don't go according to plan. ▪ Reinforce that when things go wrong and mistakes are made, you're there to give support.

Tools 25–29: Applying Observe and Reflect and Respond (ORR)

Tools 25–29: Applying Observe and Reflect and Respond (ORR)

Observe	Reflect	Respond
Is extremely active, energetic, and restless.	▪ What is my student feeling at these times? ▪ What kinds of things cause the most activity? ▪ What are the situations where he copes well?	▪ Identify times and places calm behavior is appropriate. ▪ Encourage and reinforce calming behaviors in difficult situations and help him apply and transfer the skills to less successful situations. ▪ Help him identify times/places when behavior is inappropriate by removing himself from the setting (e.g., walk away, listen to music).
Has strong, emotional recall of school experiences and peer interactions.	▪ Are the descriptions positive or negative? ▪ How and when does he share these experiences?	▪ Monitor and be aware of strong emotional reactions to situations. ▪ Find examples in literature to discuss and compare and contrast with.

Tool 29: ORR Template

Directions: Use this template to record your observations of students' actions and behaviors. Then, reflect upon and respond to your observations.

Observe	Reflect	Respond
What do I see?	**What are my questions?**	**What can I do?**

Tools 25–29: Applying Observe and Reflect and Respond (ORR)

Tool 30:
Stumbling Blocks That
Mask Strengths

Identification is complicated. Students who are bright and have learning challenges need to be carefully identified so that they can receive both the challenge and support they need and deserve. We have talked about how the lack of certain skill sets, particular behaviors, and some social/emotional issues mask the real abilities and strengths of some of our brightest students. When we look beyond these obstacles, we remove the masks that keep us from seeing the bright capabilities of these children. WORM (writing, organization, reading, and memory) is a mnemonic device we can use to help us remember four areas where many of the stumbling blocks occur.

Tips

✓ *Tool 30: Stumbling Blocks That Mask Strengths.* Twice-exceptional students have many weaknesses that mask their gifts and many strengths that mask their weaknesses. This interferes with appropriate identification. Use this checklist to identify possible stumbling blocks to identification for your student.

Tool 30: Stumbling Blocks That Mask Strengths

These students often face stumbling blocks in the areas of writing, organization, reading, and memory that mask their strengths. Check those that apply for your student.

Writing
- ❏ The physical act of putting words on paper
- ❏ Handwriting
- ❏ Generating topics
- ❏ Combining words into meaningful sentences
- ❏ Organizing sentences and incorporating adequate details and support statements into organized paragraphs
- ❏ Revising and editing
- ❏ Using language mechanics effectively (e.g., grammar, punctuation, spelling)

Organization
- ❏ Following multistep directions
- ❏ Planning the steps needed to complete a task
- ❏ Organizing desk, locker, notebook, and other materials
- ❏ Locating needed materials
- ❏ Breaking long-range assignments into manageable steps
- ❏ Prioritizing

Reading
- ❏ Decoding unfamiliar words
- ❏ Inferring meaning of new words
- ❏ Summarizing
- ❏ Reading fluently and quickly
- ❏ Using textbooks

Memory
- ❏ Concentrating and keeping track of information
- ❏ Quickly recalling details
- ❏ Retrieving details after time has passed

Keeping the Bright Turned On!

❏ **Anchors Aweigh!:** Encourage students to try something new. Set up anchor activities and centers around the room that will allow them to explore different topics on their own.

❏ **Journaling:** Have students keep a journal on the computer where they write their ideas and feelings, answering prompts like, "Today I discovered that I can . . ." or "Two things I liked about today . . ." They can also keep a running list of things to try or things to find out about.

❏ **Portfolios:** Build a portfolio of your students' work. Provide a folder/box of some kind to store work. Have the students decorate the front, showing something about themselves. Each week, have the children pick a work sample/project that they are proud of to put in the box or folder.

❏ **Acrostic Poem:** Have students create an Acrostic Poem—All About Me. They should write their name down the left side, and then think of a word that begins with each letter that describes them in some way.

❏ **Jar Joys . . . Continued!:** Have students add something that they discovered about themselves to the jar used in the previous chapter's activities.

chapter 3

How Do I Reach Them?

Failure to help the gifted child reach his potential is a societal tragedy, the extent of which is difficult to measure but what is surely great. How can we measure the sonata unwritten, the curative drug undiscovered, the absence of political insight? They are the difference between what we are and what we could be as a society.

—James J. Gallagher

Guiding Questions

❏ What are the best practices that promote success?

❏ How do I connect with these students in such a way that they are ready to learn?

Word Sparks

✓ best practices
✓ rigorous instruction
✓ strength-based instruction
✓ differentiation
✓ interventions
✓ adaptations

✓ accommodations
✓ case management
✓ learning styles
✓ roles
✓ responsibilities
✓ social/emotional

Chapter Overview

IN the previous chapters, you learned about the characteristics of bright kids with learning difficulties and methods for recognizing and understanding these students' strengths and needs. You may have informally identified a few of these students in your classroom and are now ready to begin planning for their success. In this chapter, we will discuss and respond to the question, "How do I reach them?" Although there is much to learn in order for a teacher to become a master educator of these students, you have already put a key component into place. You understand these students, you "get it." Reaching these special students academically, socially, and emotionally is about discovering and understanding them.

Four Best Practices

The primary guiding principle for teaching bright students with learning difficulties is to take a strength-based approach to applying the following four best practices.

Best Practice #1: Access to Rigorous Instruction

It is essential for these students to be encouraged to identify and develop their gifts and talents. This is the key to unlocking their potential, their self-concept, and their path through life. One way to provide access to rigorous instruction is to include these students in existing opportunities for gifted students. Some examples of these opportunities in districts around the country are gifted classrooms, pull-out programs, plug-in programs, advanced reading groups, accelerated math classes, schoolwide enrichment programs, enrichment clubs or activities, classes in local colleges, and mentor programs.

Another way for a teacher to do this is to differentiate instruction for the student based on his strengths and interests. Good teachers do not provide the same lesson to all students every day of the year. In most classrooms today, students receive whole-group lessons that address the common learning objective, but they also are instructed in small groups based on their level of readiness, interest, or learning style. They are given assignments and assessments that allow them to demonstrate their knowledge in a variety of ways through their strengths.

Working with a child's strengths puts a positive spin on learning, especially for a student who has had continued difficulty in school. For bright students with learning difficulties it is the most critical component. Instruction, when it is differentiated, better matches an individual's abilities, styles, and needs. Differentiation is a way of thinking about and planning instruction in order to meet the diverse needs of students based on their characteristics. Teachers differentiate content, process, and product according to students' readiness, interest, and learning profiles through a range of instructional and management strategies (Renzulli, 1977; Tomlinson, 1999).

To provide strength-based differentiated instruction to bright students with learning difficulties, a teacher must often extend and enrich the content, facilitate the learning process so that the student can capitalize on her strengths, and provide a variety of product options so that the student can demonstrate her knowledge while using her strengths.

Best Practice #2: Instruction and Interventions to Address the Learning Difficulties

Although development of their gifts and talents is the most important thing, it is also critical for students to improve in their areas of weakness. The primary goal for students is for them to lead productive lives and to become as independent as possible. Their lives will be much easier if they can read, write, and socialize at more proficient levels. How do we help them develop their weaker abilities? These students need instruction of skills and strategies in academic areas that are affected by their weakness or disability. The teaching of these skills and strategies is accomplished through direct instruction and/or integrated into content instruction. Instruction in this area includes helping students to develop an awareness of their strengths and weaknesses and an ability to advocate for what they need in order to be successful.

An important consideration when working on weaknesses is motivation. One way to increase intrinsic motivation for a task is by providing exciting work for students to do, thus harnessing their curiosity and passion for learning. High-interest reading material will make reluctant readers *want* to read. Assignments that allow these students to think critically and to tackle real-world problems make them *want* to get organized and to participate in the group work. Writing prompts that allow them to express their creativity and unique ideas make them *want* to write. If you engage their brains first, you will find that you can ignite their desire to learn, to create, and to express. You can then provide embedded instruction in the reading, writing, organization, and social skills that students need in order to accomplish the desired task. If you take an isolated approach to remediation, you will often find these students unwilling participants in their learning.

Best Practice #3: Instructional Adaptations and Accommodations

For twice-exceptional students to effectively gain access to enriched and accelerated instruction, they often need to have appropriate adaptations and accommodations (Barton & Starnes, 1989; Baum, Owen, & Dixon, 1991; Cline & Schwartz, 1999). Accommodations allow bright students with learning challenges to demonstrate their knowledge without being handicapped by the effects of their difficulties. These accommodations can run the gamut from a seat at the front of the classroom to a scribe for writing assignments.

When considering adaptations and accommodations, there are several overarching principles that should be considered. First, accommodations should be based on the strengths of the student. For example, if you have a very verbal student who cannot write, then a dictation accommodation (or use of voice-to-text software such as Dragon Naturally Speaking) might be appropriate. But if you have a student who cannot give an organized dictated response, that accommodation won't work very well. Secondly, provision of accommodations is something you must plan for and should not be something the student must request. Also, accommodations are intended to move students, over time and as much as possible, from dependence to independence. With that in mind, an accommodation that is appropriate at a given point in time may be replaced at a later time with another one that helps the student to be more independent.

Additionally, the decisions regarding adaptations must be individualized for each student, those used in assessments must parallel those used in instruction, and they must provide an equal opportunity for students to demonstrate their knowledge. Lastly, accommodations must be evaluated often, and only those that are effective should be continued (Weinfeld et al., 2006).

Best Practice #4: Case Management and Social/Emotional Support

These students need to be provided with a balanced instructional day that includes advanced instruction and intervention. Throughout the day they require many individualized accommodations to be provided systematically and consistently. It often requires a team approach to get to this level of coordinated programming. The bright child with learning difficulties often has many teachers and adults working with him throughout the day, including (but not limited to) the gifted program teacher, the special educator, instructional assistants, the counselor, the art and music teachers, the media specialist, a coach, and his parents. All of these people need to have an awareness and understanding of that student's strengths and needs, and they need to be on the same page with accommodations and supports. Therefore, it is necessary for an individual on the team to assume the role of case manager. This person's job is to coordinate the overall programming for the student, to facilitate communication regarding the student, and to be the go-to person for that student.

Additionally, these students often require some social/emotional support to stay afloat. This support can come in a variety of ways, but we've found the following things to be necessary for most students. First, they need someone to explain to them about their personal strengths and needs. These kids generally know that something is wrong and they don't quite believe us when we just tell them they are smart. They are often relieved when we demystify their learning difficulty and also show and tell them specifically *how* they are smart. A realistic understanding of their strengths and weaknesses is a critical first step to self-awareness and eventual self-acceptance. Second, these students benefit incredibly from spending time with other students like them. If at all possible, forming small (mixed-age, if necessary) groups of bright students with learning problems to meet periodically to work together on projects of interest and/or to talk about common issues really helps these students become proud of who they are. Finding an older student to mentor a younger student with a similar profile is also a wonderful way to accomplish this goal. Meeting people like them lets them know they are not alone and is often a great way for them to finally make a friend with common interests. Third, these students may need direct emotional supports. The school frustration and sense of isolation they experience often leads to feelings of worry or sadness. Specialized instruction devoted to developing coping strategies and a positive self-concept are helpful for these students. Just knowing they can visit a trusted adult and talk when they are nervous or upset is often a great source of comfort.

Designing a Complete Program of Instruction for the Student: Intervention Plans

When it is suspected that a student is bright or gifted and has learning challenges, it is crucial that the adults who are involved come together with the student to analyze his strengths and needs and then together create an appropriate intervention plan that provides for programming and supports in each of the four best practices. Creating this plan calls first for careful analysis of a student's strengths as well as challenges. Next, the current programming and supports are evaluated to see what is already in place and what is lacking. Finally, recommendations are made for program changes. The key is to provide a balanced instructional program for the student that emphasizes nurturing and developing his strengths while simultaneously remediating and supporting his weaker areas.

Student Profiles

Now let's take a look at what a balanced instructional program with an emphasis on the student's strengths could look like for Sarah, Jeremy, and Darryl.

Sarah

Here are a few questions Sarah's teachers may be struggling to answer:

- Do I move her up to the advanced math class or not?

- How can I help her to connect to text so that she can participate in class discussions at a level consistent with her ability?
- How can I help her be a better writer? How can I help her enjoy writing?
- What organizational supports will help her? How do I get her to use these supports?

Access to Rigorous Instruction

Sarah is in a math class that is working on curriculum 2 years above grade level. She is in the gifted reading group that uses language arts units developed by the Center for Gifted Education at the College of William and Mary, and the teacher provides her with novel choices so that she can select books of interest. With this as the hook, Sarah is able to absorb the text and participate in interpretive discussions about the text. She is in the science club and is working hard on her inquiry project that she will share with her classmates and potentially enter into the schoolwide science fair.

Instruction and Interventions to Address the Learning Difficulties

Sarah is in a pull-out writing group taught by a special educator. He instructs her small group in specific skills using the 6+1 Traits of Writing as the means for breaking down the complex task of writing. He supports Sarah's development and use of writing process strategies by working with her on writing assignments from her language arts teacher. He has taught her to use brainstorming strategies to generate possible ideas. She has learned to select and narrow her topic and then to develop her ideas fully by first conferencing verbally with an adult. Recently, she has begun using the computer-based webbing software Inspiration to capture and organize her ideas. Using all of these strategies, she is then typically able to write her first draft fairly independently.

The special educator also pulls her out once a week to introduce her to a variety of organizational techniques and strategies to help Sarah better organize her time and materials. Together they decide what would work best for Sarah given her learning style and personal preferences. These decisions are then communicated to all other teachers and to her parents, who will support Sarah's use of these strategies. The team has found that by giving Sarah choice in this area, she is more willing to follow through and to buy into these organizational supports.

Instructional Adaptations and Accommodations

At the beginning of each day, Sarah's teacher touches base with her to get her ready for a good day. She shares any unexpected changes to the routine/schedule and cues Sarah to go through her morning checklist. At the end of each day, the teacher reviews Sarah's assignment planner with her and goes through her materials to ensure that everything is in its proper place and that she understands her homework. All of Sarah's teachers provide her with individual cues and prompting, with a seat toward the front of the room, with frequent breaks, and with alternative means of demonstrating her knowledge. To aid in her memory and comprehension of the novels, she is asked to create a storyboard of each chapter that she can refer to during class discussions and for writing assignments. Sarah's math teacher gives her grid paper folded into quarters on which to organize her problems so they don't run all over the page. She also reduces Sarah's workload, focusing on the more challenging problems, and has taught Sarah how to explain her thinking using words, symbols, and illustrations. When she doesn't know how Sarah arrived at an answer, she asks her to tell her verbally using prompts to organize her thinking such as, "What did you do first? Then? Next?"

Case-Management and Social-Emotional Support

Sarah's team meets quarterly to discuss her progress and to refine the supports in place for her. Her special education case manager initiates weekly e-mails to the teachers to check her progress. Sarah's teachers also use e-mail to communicate information to the case manager and to Sarah and her parents regarding daily assignments and issues. She occasionally uses her "flash pass" to leave the classroom to talk to the counselor when specific issues crop up throughout the day. They problem solve and discuss her use of previously taught coping strategies to reduce her feelings of frustration and anxiety. Problems and issues have significantly decreased since the implementation of the four best practices.

Jeremy

Here are a few questions Jeremy's teachers may be struggling to answer:

- Will I put him in the teacher-led, on-level social studies group or in the enrichment group, where he will need to work more independently and cooperatively?

- How do I challenge him in reading while also helping him improve in the area of reading comprehension?
- How do I help Jeremy increase his social competency and develop friendships?
- What do I do to avoid Jeremy's meltdowns?

Access to Rigorous Instruction

Jeremy is in the advanced math class working 1 year above grade level. He participates in the science and social studies enrichment groups, and his teacher has developed an anchor project for him that he can work on when he already knows (or learns quickly) the materials they are covering that day. Jeremy participates in higher level reading groups and small-group instruction utilizing *Jacob's Ladder*, a program designed to help students bring their reading comprehension from the literal to inferential levels. The goal is that he will participate in Junior Great Books instruction with support next year.

Instruction and Interventions to Address the Learning Difficulties

The school counselor sees Jeremy weekly one-on-one and also in weekly social skills groups. In their one-on-one sessions she uses social stories, rule cards, and other methods to explicitly teach him social skills that he is lacking and coping skills to deal with his anxiety and frustration. In the weekly group, he has the opportunity to apply and practice these skills in a structured and supported setting. The counselor communicates the nature and progress of their work to the rest of the team so that they can also support Jeremy's use of strategies and practice of skills in other settings. The special educator plugs into Jeremy's writing classroom three times each week to teach him writing strategies, to support his use of technology, and to guide him through the writing process with class assignments. Jeremy's reading teacher provides direct, explicit instruction in nonliteral language and characterization to support his comprehension of literature (e.g., "Sam feels sad because his puppy is lost," "It's raining cats and dogs means it was raining very hard").

Instructional Adaptations and Accommodations

Jeremy is given specific tasks and roles for group work, and the teachers carefully assign him tasks that he is capable of doing well, while at the same time continuing to offer rigor and challenge instructionally. Rules and expectations are posted and referred to frequently throughout the day. Teachers maintain consistent routines and attempt to create a predictable schedule for Jeremy. They have created a visual schedule for him that he carries with him throughout the day, checking off activities as they are completed. They give him advance notice of changes and transitions so that he is ready for them.

Case-Management and Social-Emotional Support

Jeremy has a behavior contract that targets current issues in a positive reinforcement format. He earns tokens frequently throughout the day that he can accumulate and use to purchase desired items through his personal store. Some of the incentives used are praise, time to work on his science or social studies anchor activity, time to talk to his favorite teachers, time on the computer, food items, or items from the classroom prize bin. When Jeremy is feeling stressed, he can use his flash pass to go see the school counselor. Jeremy's case manager maintains close communication with the team and parents via e-mail and the telephone. They have a standing meeting once a month but lately, since implementation of the plan described here, there haven't been any concerns that required them to meet formally.

Darryl

Here are a few questions Darryl's teachers may be struggling to answer:

- How can I improve Darryl's reading and writing skills so that he can be more independent in the classroom?
- Should Darryl be in the advanced reading group based on his listening comprehension level or in the low reading group based on his independent reading level?
- How do I help Darryl see his strengths and improve his self-esteem?

Access to Rigorous Instruction

Darryl is in the advanced math class, has an individual enrichment project that he works on with a special educator, participates in the William and Mary and Junior Great Books reading programs with the gifted teacher, and participates in the afterschool chess club. Darryl's teachers connect his interests to the curriculum and give him many opportunities to show what he knows orally through dictation and oral presentations and by using technology.

Instruction and Interventions to Address the Learning Difficulties

Darryl is pulled out by a special educator 4–5 times a week to receive reading intervention using the Wilson Reading Program. During morning work, Darryl spends 15 minutes on a typing program or on a computer-based reading fluency program (alternate days). Darryl participates in explicit, small-group writing instruction during the writing block using the 6+1 Traits of Writing program.

Instructional Adaptations and Accommodations

Darryl receives reading support either from an adult, a peer, or using technology (e.g., recorded books, Kurzweil 3000 software). He uses a word processor with word prediction software to support his handwriting and spelling. The teacher verbally conferences with Darryl throughout the writing process to give him "talk-it-through" opportunities to develop his ideas. Darryl gets a copy of class notes to supplement his own notes. The math teacher reduces his homework load so that Darryl is able to demonstrate his knowledge with fewer problems.

Case-Management and Social-Emotional Support

Darryl's team meets monthly to discuss his progress, and his case manager, the special education teacher, communicates frequently with his parents. His case manager and the counselor meet with Darryl and other twice-exceptional students in the building in monthly sessions focused on self-awareness and self-advocacy. His classroom teacher holds a special weekly lunch bunch with the same group of kids where they eat and discuss topics of interest or concern and then work on group art projects.

Chapter Conclusion

Now that you have an understanding of the strength-based approach to the four best practices to ensure students' success, you are ready to explore this chapter's tools. These tools will support you as you strive to provide instruction that is sensitive and responsive to twice-exceptional students' strengths and weaknesses. The tools that follow will help you to tailor an appropriate program for individual students who fit this profile.

Tool 31:
Strength-Based Instruction

Working through a child's strengths puts a positive spin on learning, especially for a student who has had continued difficulty in school. Help your students be aware of their own strengths and how they learn best. Provide opportunities for them to share this information with you and their parents so that they can receive the type of instruction that they need and ultimately do their best and be successful. Differentiated instruction better matches an individual's abilities, styles, and needs.

Tips

✓ *Tool 31: Part of My Plan.* Use this tool as a self-evaluation regarding best practices for bright students with learning difficulties who need to have these components in place in order to be successful. Consider these elements as you plan lessons and offer ways for students to demonstrate understanding.

Tool 31: Part of My Plan

Directions: Listed below are ways to provide strength-based instruction. Think about the past week or month and reflect on the instruction that you provided to your class. On a scale of 1, meaning "I'm just beginning," to 5, meaning "It is always part of my plan," mark where you are. Revisit the chart often to see how you are doing.

Present instruction addressing students' learning styles.	1 2 3 4 5
Use a multisensory (visual, spatial, musical, artistic, kinesthetic) approach when introducing concepts.	1 2 3 4 5
Provide open-ended projects so that students can complete assignments through multiple outlets.	1 2 3 4 5
Provide activities that focus on students' individual gifts and interests.	1 2 3 4 5
Differentiate content by increasing complexity and offering a variety of materials.	1 2 3 4 5
Differentiate process by offering a variety of tasks and activities to support learning of content.	1 2 3 4 5
Differentiate products by offering students alternative ways to show what they know.	1 2 3 4 5
Have students engage in real-life tasks.	1 2 3 4 5
Provide hands-on experiences.	1 2 3 4 5
Provide opportunities for students to create and present their original ideas and work.	1 2 3 4 5
Integrate visual and performing arts into instruction.	1 2 3 4 5
Make technology available at all times.	1 2 3 4 5

Note. Adapted from Tomlinson (2000).

Tool 31: Strength-Based Instruction

Tools 32–35:
Learning Styles

Children learn and process information in different ways. Researchers like Kenneth and Rita Dunn, who have studied learning styles since 1967 (see Dunn, Dunn, & Treffinger, 1992, for an example of their work), have contributed to our understanding about the ways that learners concentrate on, process, and retain new and difficult information. Our challenge is to find ways to uncover how children approach learning and help them be successful learners by using their strengths. We can teach children at home and at school through their individual learning style preferences and strengths. Our observations, reflections, and responses to children's behaviors give us insights we can use. Teachers and parents should support and encourage the learner's style in order to help children compensate for skills with which they may struggle (Ricci et al., 2006).

Tips

✓ *Tool 32: Student Tool: I've Got Style!* Learn more about the different learning style preferences of your students by having them complete this activity. When processing their responses, talk about how they can use their strengths at school.

✓ *Tool 33: Learning Style Checklist.* Use this tool to record your students' learning styles.

✓ *Tool 34: Lessons With Style!* Use as a tool when planning instruction to incorporate all four of the learning styles.

✓ *Tool 35: Parent Partnership Piece: Learning Styles.* Share the information about learning styles with parents.

Tool 32: Student Tool
I've Got Style!

Directions: How do you learn best? Read each option below and check your preference. If your preference is not listed, write to the side what works for you.

If I had to put together a model airplane, I would rather:

_____ listen to the directions (A)   or   _____ read them myself (V)

If I had to learn facts about the Revolutionary War, I would rather:

_____ watch a video (V)   or   _____ participate in a reenactment (K)

If I had to learn about culture in the 1940s, I would rather:

_____ listen to music (A)   or   _____ view a piece of artwork (V)

If I had to know how to recycle, I would rather:

_____ visit a recycling plant (K)   or   _____ watch a demonstration (V)

If I had to understand how electric circuits work, I would rather:

_____ make one with my hands (T)   or   _____ listen to an explanation (A)

If I had to help with the school play, I would rather:

_____ build the scenery (T)   or   _____ have an acting role (K)

If I had to research a topic, I would rather:

_____ interview/listen to an   or   _____ go to a museum (K)
expert (A)

Did you have lots of "A" responses? You might be an **auditory learner!**

Did you have lots of "V" responses? You might be a **visual learner!**

Did you have lots of "K" responses? You might be a **kinesthetic learner!**

Did you have lots of "T" responses? You might be a **tactile learner!**

Tool 33: Learning Style Checklist

Directions: Based on your own observations and results from Tool 32, record the learning style preferences of your students.

Learning Style Preference	Description	Student Names and Notes
Visual	Learn by seeing	
Auditory	Learn by listening	
Kinesthetic	Learn by moving	
Tactile	Learn by touching	

Tools 32–35: Learning Styles

Tool 34: Lessons With Style!

Directions: Consider the learning styles of all of your students. Use this template as a way to ensure that your lesson incorporates ways of reaching all of the learning styles. In this template, Process refers to how you'll teach these types of learners, while Product refers to how they will show you what they have learned.

For the Auditory Learner

Process

Product

For the Visual Learner

Process

Product

The Lesson

Concepts/Objectives:

For the Tactile Learner

Process

Product

For the Kinesthetic Learner

Process

Product

Tool 35: Parent Partnership Piece
Learning Styles

Dear Parent,

In class, we have done exercises and activities to help your child be able to answer the following questions: What kind of learner am I? How do I learn best?

Children learn and process information in different ways and have preferences in how they like to learn. Our challenge is to find ways to uncover how children approach learning and help them be successful learners by using their strengths. Some children learn by hearing (auditory learners), some learn by moving their bodies (kinesthetic learners), some learn by seeing (visual learners), and some learn by touching (tactile learners). Auditory learners, who hear and remember what is taught, may learn the alphabet through song. Kinesthetic learners may make letters by using their whole bodies. Tactile learners may learn the alphabet by tracing letters in sand at a sensory table. Visual learners may recognize the alphabet on flashcards.

We can teach children at home and at school through their individual learning styles. Our observations, reflections, and responses to children's behaviors give us insights we can use. Teachers and parents should support and encourage the learner's style (teaching to the strength) in order to help a child compensate for skills with which he or she may struggle.

Knowing your child's learning style will help us understand how your child learns best. Based on what you know about your child's learning preferences, please answer the attached questions and return them to me. The information that I learn about the way your child works at home and his or her preferences for different types of work will help me better plan for him or her in school.

Sincerely,

How My Child Learns Best

1. What type of environment does your child prefer when learning something new or doing homework? A quiet place with little distraction? Background music? At the kitchen table with you nearby? In his or her bedroom with the door shut?

_____

_____

_____

_____

2. Does your child sit and complete work or does he or she need to get up and move around?

_____

_____

_____

_____

3. When learning new material, does your child need to say things out loud? Hear them as well as see them? Write down notes?

_____

_____

_____

_____

4. Tell me about a recent assignment or time when your child became totally engaged in learning.

_____

_____

_____

_____

5. When interested in a topic, where does your child go to seek information (e.g., the library, the Internet, direct experiences, television programs, interviewing others, books)?

_____

_____

_____

_____

6. Based on what you have observed about your child, what type of learner do you think your child is (visual, auditory, kinesthetic, or tactile)?

_____

_____

_____

_____

Tools 32–35: Learning Styles

Tools 36 and 37: Differentiation

A challenge teachers constantly face when planning instruction is knowing exactly how much challenge to provide students so that they are engaged but not frustrated. This can be even more difficult when you are working with bright students with learning difficulties, as they are often frustrated by their inability to keep up with their peers. At the same time, providing challenging opportunities in which they can be successful helps them gain self-confidence and self-esteem. Knowing what challenges each student and what causes her frustration will help you plan the optimal match. Use the following tools as an informal way to gather information about how your students learn best, their preferred learning styles, what your students consider challenging, and what may frustrate them.

Tips

✓ *Tool 36: Differentiation Checklist.* Differentiated instruction better matches an individual's abilities, styles, and needs. Use this tool to evaluate how your instruction is differentiated.

✓ *Tool 37: Student Tool: The Quest for the Optimal Match.* Have your students think about the types of activities/subjects that they enjoy. Do they prefer activities that are easy for them or ones that present a challenge? What activities do they find too difficult and therefore avoid? Some people prefer to do things that are a little hard, but not too hard, because it provides them with a sense of accomplishment.

Tool 36: Differentiation Checklist

Directions: Use the following checklist as you plan and implement differentiation within your classroom. This is not a complete list, but rather a starting point.

_____ Use a variety of assessments to discover what students know, including test data, pretests, writing samples, discussions, observations, products, and parent and student input.

_____ Provide positive expectations and respect for individual differences.

_____ Support strength-based instruction in content, process, and product.

_____ Provide for acceleration and enrichment.

_____ Provide appropriate adaptations and accommodations.

_____ Integrate basic skills and higher level questioning and thinking in the curriculum.

_____ Provide opportunities for critical and creative thinking.

_____ Provide a variety of classroom resources and materials with several levels of difficulty.

_____ Provide flexible grouping.

_____ Provide for guided and independent work.

_____ Offer a variety of activities and allow for student choice.

_____ Provide for alternative products to allow students to show what they know.

_____ Allow students to make decisions about creating and presenting original topics.

_____ Use a variety of assistive technology tools.

_____ Help students monitor and evaluate their own work.

_____ Use varied, stimulating, and performance-based assessments.

Tools 36 and 37: Differentiation

Tool 37: Student Tool
The Quest for the Optimal Match

Tools 36 and 37: Differentiation

| Things that I like that are challenging: | Things that are easy for me but boring: |
| Things that I find frustrating: | Things that are easy but fun to do: |

Tools 38 and 39: Adaptations and Accommodations

For students who are gifted and have learning disabilities to participate and succeed in enriched and accelerated instruction, they often need to have appropriate adaptations and accommodations (Barton & Starnes, 1989; Baum et al., 1991; Cline & Schwartz, 1999; National Association for Gifted Children [NAGC], 1998). Many accommodations allow bright students with learning challenges to demonstrate their knowledge without being handicapped by the effects of their difficulties. In planning, it is crucial that the teacher consider instructional methods and strategies that either circumvent the student's difficulties or that build the necessary scaffolding to empower students to be successful with the demands of the assignment.

Tips

✓ *Tool 38: Adaptations and Accommodations Checklist.* Consider these best practices for selecting and evaluating accommodations with your team when developing or revising accommodations for students with disabilities.

✓ *Tool 39: Parent Partnership Piece: Adaptations and Accommodations.* Send home the parent letter to parents of students receiving formal accommodations through an IEP or 504 Plan prior to any meeting where their child's accommodations are going to be reviewed. The letter will help parents understand best practices for selecting and evaluating adaptations and accommodations.

Tool 38: Adaptations and Accommodations Checklist

The following principles are best practices for providing appropriate adaptations and accommodations to students. Comprehensive explanations of each item can be found in the book *Smart Kids With Learning Difficulties* (Weinfeld et al., 2006).

_____ Accommodations used in assessments should parallel accommodations that are integrated into classroom instruction (Council for Exceptional Children [CEC], 2000; Maryland State Department of Education [MSDE], 2000).

_____ The adaptations/accommodations are aligned with the educational impact of the individual student's disability and the adaptations/accommodations are aligned with the needs described in the student's IEP or 504 Plan (CEC, 2000; MSDE, 2000).

_____ The adaptations/accommodations are based upon the strengths of the student (Baum et al., 1991; Gardner, 1983; NAGC, 1998).

_____ Accommodations are based on what students need in order to be provided with an equal opportunity to show what they know without impediment of their disability (Thurlow, House, Scott, & Ysseldyke, 2001).

_____ Assessments allow students, while using appropriate accommodations, to demonstrate their skills without the interference of their disabilities (CEC, 2000).

_____ After selecting and providing appropriate adaptations/accommodations, their impact on the performance of the individual student is evaluated and only those that are effective are continued (Fuchs, Fuchs, Eaton, Hamlett, & Karns, 2000).

_____ The adaptations/accommodations are reviewed, revised, and when appropriate, faded over time, allowing the student to move from dependence to independence (MSDE, 2000).

_____ A multidisciplinary team, which considers the input of the parent and student, decides upon the adaptations/accommodations (IDEA, 1997; Section 504, 1973).

_____ The appropriate adaptations/accommodations and the rationale for each of them are shared with all staff members who work with the student (IDEA, 1997).

Tool 39: Parent Partnership Piece
Adaptations and Accommodations

Dear Parent,

Accommodations are provided to bright students with learning challenges to allow them to demonstrate their knowledge without being limited by the effects of their disabilities. As you know, we will be meeting soon as a team to review your child's progress and educational plan. Part of that review will include revising your child's accommodations. Look over the information below based on best practices for selecting and evaluating accommodations for students with disabilities. You also may want to review your child's current accommodations with him or her. Bring your thoughts and ideas regarding what's working well and any additions or changes you would like to propose to the meeting. Remember:

- Accommodations used on tests and quizzes should also be used during instruction on a regular basis.
- The adaptations/accommodations must address the needs of your child and be necessary to allow him or her access to appropriately challenging instruction.
- The adaptations/accommodations are based upon the strengths of your child.
- Accommodations are based on what your child needs in order to be provided with an equal opportunity (as opposed to an unfair advantage) to show what he or she knows without impediment of his or her disability.
- Accommodations allow your child to demonstrate his or her skills and knowledge without the interference of the disabilities.
- Adaptations/accommodations should be evaluated periodically and only those that are effective should be continued.
- Adaptations/accommodations should allow your child to move from dependence to independence. Accommodations that are no longer needed are removed over time.
- A multidisciplinary team, which considers the input of the parent and student, decides upon the adaptations/accommodations.
- The appropriate adaptations/accommodations and the rationale for each of them are shared with all staff members who work with the student.

After reviewing this information and your child's current accommodations, let me know if you have any questions or concerns.

Sincerely,

Tools 38 and 39: Adaptations and Accommodations

Tool 40:
Adaptations/Accommodations for Overcoming Obstacles Checklist

Once obstacles to learning have been identified, it is critical to select accommodations that allow the student to be successful. The checklists in this section provide suggestions for appropriate adaptations and accommodations that obviate student weaknesses related to the obstacles of writing, organization, reading, and memory. They are listed in the following subcategories: Assistive Technology, Instructional Materials, and Teaching/Assessment Methods.

Tips

✓ *Tool 40: Adaptations/Accommodations for Overcoming Obstacles Checklist* (Montgomery County Public Schools, 2004). Use the ideas when planning and implementing strategies for overcoming obstacles. Share with parents or ask for their input when discussing and selecting accommodations. Use with the student when conferencing and working on *Tool 43: What's in My Toolbox?*

Tool 40: Adaptations/Accommodations for Overcoming Obstacles Checklist

Adaptations/Accommodations for Overcoming Obstacles Related to Writing

Assistive Technology	Instructional Materials	Teaching/Assessment Methods
<ul><li>use voice recognition software</li><li>use writing organizational software</li><li>use electronic spellers and dictionaries</li><li>use computer word processors with spelling and grammar checkers or talking capabilities</li><li>use portable keyboards</li><li>use word prediction software</li><li>use programs that allow writing to be read aloud to provide for audio spell check, proofreading, word prediction, and homophone distinction</li><li>use tape recorder or voice recorder for transcription after student dictation</li></ul>	<ul><li>use step-by-step written directions</li><li>use a proofreading checklist</li><li>use scoring rubrics, models, and anchor papers for students to evaluate their own work</li><li>use graphic organizers</li><li>use guides such as story starters, webs, story charts, and outlines</li><li>use dictionaries, word banks, and thesauruses</li><li>use personal dictionaries of misused and misspelled words</li><li>use highlighters to indicate errors/corrections</li><li>use copy of teacher's notes or of another student's notes (No Carbon Required [NCR] paper)</li><li>use pencil grips</li><li>use paper with raised lines</li><li>use mechanical pencils</li><li>use slant boards</li></ul>	<ul><li>focus on content rather than mechanics</li><li>focus on quality rather than quantity</li><li>prepare storyboards, guided imagery, dramatization, or projects before the writing process</li><li>set an important purpose for writing, such as writing for publication, writing to an expert, or writing to a famous person</li><li>allow students to write in their areas of interest or expertise</li><li>provide a multiple intelligences approach</li><li>allow students to demonstrate understanding through alternative ways/products</li><li>reduce or alter written requirements</li><li>break down assignments into smaller, manageable parts</li><li>allow additional time</li><li>permit work with partners or small groups to confer for revising, editing, and proofreading</li><li>proofread for one type of error at a time</li><li>permit words or phrases instead of complete sentences</li><li>provide artistic (visual, spatial, and performing) products to communicate knowledge</li><li>provide scientific and technological products to communicate knowledge</li><li>provide dictated response to a person or tape recorder</li><li>provide a portfolio assessment of products and performances as well as grading writing products</li><li>allow alternative spelling</li><li>allow manuscript, cursive, or typewritten work</li></ul>

Tool 40: Adaptations/Accommodations for Overcoming Obstacles Checklist

Adaptations/Accommodations for Overcoming
Obstacles Related to Organization

Assistive Technology	Instructional Materials	Teaching/Assessment Methods
▪ use electronic organizers ▪ use software organization programs ▪ tape record assignments ▪ e-mail assignments from school to students' home accounts	▪ use visual models, storyboards, Venn diagrams, matrices, and flow charts ▪ use study guides that assist with locating information and answers ▪ use highlighters, index tabs, and colored stickers ▪ use assignment books and calendars for recording assignments ▪ use outlines, webs, diagrams, and other graphic organizers	▪ use short, simple directions ▪ provide advanced organizers regarding what students will know by the end of the lesson ▪ post class and homework assignments in the same area each day and make sure that students record them and/or have a printed copy ▪ verbally review class and homework assignments ▪ list and verbally review step-by-step directions for assignments ▪ work with students to establish specific due dates for short assignments and time frames for long-term assignments ▪ break up tasks into workable and obtainable steps ▪ give examples and specific steps to accomplish tasks ▪ provide checkpoints for long-term assignments and monitor progress frequently ▪ allow students to review and summarize important information and directions ▪ utilize a multisensory or multiple intelligences approach to teaching organizational skills ▪ invite student questions regarding directions and assignments ▪ provide students with a list of needed materials and their locations ▪ periodically check notebooks and lockers ▪ make time to organize materials and assignments ▪ encourage study buddies ▪ provide a homework hotline or structured homework assistance ▪ post a daily routine and explain any changes in that routine ▪ provide an uncluttered work area ▪ label and store materials in designated locations ▪ provide a specific location for students to place completed work ▪ provide samples of finished products ▪ allow artistic products to communicate knowledge ▪ allow scientific and technological products to communicate knowledge ▪ allow dictated responses to a person or tape recorder ▪ provide a portfolio assessment of products and performances as well as grading writing products ▪ allow alternative spelling ▪ allow manuscript, cursive, or typewritten work

Tool 40: Adaptations/Accommodations for Overcoming Obstacles Checklist

Adaptations/Accommodations for Overcoming Obstacles Related to Reading

Assistive Technology	Instructional Materials	Teaching/Assessment Methods
▪ use CD-ROMs with an audio component ▪ use electronic spellers that speak words aloud ▪ use books on tape and digital books ▪ use computer programs that allow words to be read aloud ▪ use text-to-speech software	▪ use primary sources such as interviews, guest speakers, and demonstrations ▪ use multimedia presentations ▪ use tape-recorded directions or tests ▪ use text study guides and graphic organizers to help students locate information ▪ use high-interest, appropriate reading level material and multilevel texts about the same topic ▪ use above-grade-level, high-interest reading material ▪ use rich literature experiences ▪ provide access to challenging programs, like curriculum created by the College of William and Mary's Center for Gifted Education and the Junior Great Books program ▪ use expository reading experiences ▪ use visuals (e.g., outlines, advanced organizers, graphic organizers, charts, photographs, diagrams, and maps) to aid in understanding written information ▪ use word banks	▪ develop interest and curiosity by activating prior knowledge before reading ▪ use a multiple intelligences approach ▪ begin with an experience or project ▪ teach through the arts (e.g., drama, visual arts, poetry) ▪ utilize simulations and moral dilemmas ▪ encourage reading related to students' areas of interest ▪ set purposes for reading and state what students should know after reading the text ▪ ask lower level comprehension questions in order to build up to higher level questions ▪ cue students to important words and concepts verbally and through highlighting ▪ teach vocabulary in context ▪ give students the opportunity to read silently before reading aloud ▪ allow students to choose whether or not to read aloud ▪ pair students who have strong decoding skills with weak decoders ▪ allow students to do vocabulary webs, literature webs, and other difficult tasks in small groups ▪ read directions or tests aloud ▪ allow additional time for reading ▪ teach students to outline, underline, or highlight important points in reading ▪ encourage students to take notes while reading ▪ offer support and clarification for imbedded directions in text

Tool 40: Adaptations/Accommodations for Overcoming Obstacles Checklist

Adaptations/Accommodations for Overcoming Obstacles Related to Memory

Assistive Technology	Instructional Materials	Teaching/Assessment Methods
▪ have teachers use software programs as an alternative or additional way of presenting information ▪ have students tape or digitally record directions or information ▪ have students use software programs for organization of key points ▪ add notes about directions or key points as part of assignments given on the computer	▪ use multiple modalities, including art and simulations when presenting directions, explanations, and instructional content ▪ use a multiple intelligences approach ▪ utilize materials that are meaningful to students ▪ provide students with copies of the information that highlights key facts	▪ have students repeat the directions or information back to the teacher ▪ have students repeat information to themselves ▪ repeat the information or directions to the students ▪ reinforce details ▪ have students recall important details at the end of a lesson or period of time ▪ have students sequence activities after a lesson or event ▪ have students teach information to other students through demonstration or explanation, not tutoring ▪ have students deliver the schedule of events to other students ▪ deliver directions, explanations, and instructional content in a clear manner and at an appropriate pace ▪ provide students with environmental cues and prompts such as posted rules and steps for performing tasks ▪ provide students with a written list of materials and directions ▪ have students use resources in the environment to recall information (e.g., notes, textbooks, pictures) ▪ give auditory and visual cues to help students to recall information ▪ relate information presented to students' previous experiences ▪ have students outline, highlight, underline, or summarize information that should be remembered ▪ provide adequate opportunities for repetition of information through different experiences and modalities ▪ provide students with information from a variety of sources ▪ tell students what to listen for when being given directions or receiving information ▪ have students use advanced organizers ▪ use visual imagery

Tools 41 and 42: What's Possible? The Sky's the Limit!

Having students focus on their strengths and successes helps increase self-concept and build self-confidence. Just as important is having students begin to recognize their areas of need and figure out what they need to be successful. Working on these two areas simultaneously will help students gain a better understanding of who they are as learners. At the same time, you will gain information that will help you plan your instruction. Conferencing with the students lets them know that you are there for them and truly care that they are successful.

Tips

✓ *Tool 41: Student Tool: The "I Can" Attitude!* Encourage students to use the tool to record successes as they occur. In the beginning, you may need to point out achievements and suggest that they record them. Pick the format that best fits your students, or have them develop their own record-keeping sheet. Have students reflect on what went right and what worked. Set up conference times to review the successes and discuss what worked or what helped. Help students think of ways to apply what worked to other areas and/or situations.

✓ *Tool 42: Student Tool: Ticket to Talk.* This tool offers students a non-threatening way to begin to discuss their areas of need with you. It also introduces the idea of self-advocacy. Make the forms available somewhere in the room or provide copies for students to keep in their desks.

Tool 41: Student Tool
The "I Can" Attitude!

This is a place to record your achievements, big and small! Have you ever heard anyone say, "Learn from your mistakes"? Well, it is just as important to learn from your successes! When you achieve something that may have been particularly difficult, it's a great feeling, right?

Directions: Look over the example provided. When you have an accomplishment that you are proud of, take the time to reflect on "what worked." Using the blank chart, record your success, list what worked, and think of ways you can use what worked in other situations! You can draw pictures of what worked for you if you prefer. You may want to ask your teacher or parent to help you figure out what worked and why.

A success that I had!	What worked? What helped?	If I could do that, then maybe I could . . .
Example: I got an "A" on my paragraph	I talked about my ideas with a friend first and put my ideas on sticky notes.	Try to record my ideas before I start to write, so I can go back to them. Write my ideas on sticky notes so I can move them around and order them before I start writing.

A success that I had!	What worked? What helped?	If I could do that, then maybe I could . . .

Tools 41 and 42: What's Possible? The Sky's the Limit!

Tools 41 and 42: What's Possible? The Sky's the Limit!

Tool 42: Student Tool
Ticket to Talk

I had trouble with my
_____ assignment.

I would like to have a conference with
you to get some help.

Student's name_____

TICKET

- -

Let's Talk!

Meeting time/place: _____

Teacher signature: _____

Tool 43:
What's in My Toolbox?

Although the IEP team is ultimately responsible for determining the appropriate accommodations that are put in place for a student, the student needs to agree and be willing to use the accommodations in order for them to be effective. Not all accommodations are equally necessary or effective with all tasks. The accommodation(s) needed will vary depending on the task and how the student is progressing and feeling on that given day. This tool will serve as a menu of tried-and-true accommodations that work for that student. As your student builds on the tools in the toolbox that work, you and/or the student can share the information with other teachers, which will help the student to build his self-advocacy skills.

Tips

✓ *Tool 43: What's in My Toolbox?* This tool will help you to develop a menu of accommodations that are effective for your student. Use it with your student to reflect on a difficult assignment(s). Discuss the obstacles that got in the way of him or her being successful. Ask what might help for next time. Use Tool 40 as a reference. Together, select accommodation(s) that will work for him or her on a particular assignment by looking back at the menu. Have the student also add the accommodations that worked from Tool 41.

Tool 43: Student Tool
What's in My Toolbox?
Exploring My Options

Directions: Consider recent assignments that have been difficult for you. In the first column of the chart below, identify what gets in your way (such as writing, organizing, reading, remembering, listening, attending, or making good choices). Then, meet with your teacher and in the second column, record ideas of what could help you. Try the ideas. See what works. If it was helpful, put a check by it under "It's a Keeper!" See the example below.

What Got in My Way?	Things That May Help Me (Possible Accommodations to Try)	It's a Keeper! Add it to My Toolbox
I couldn't finish the reading in time	Use books on tape Read with a buddy Break down the reading and do a little bit each night Ask for it ahead of time	✓ ✓

Tool 43: What's in My Toolbox?

Tools 44 and 45:
Bordering on Excellence Tools

The Bordering on Excellence tools drive theory to practice by helping teachers tailor instruction for each student. They interface with any instructional material and will allow educators to consider the multiple issues that they need to effectively and efficiently address when differentiating content, process, and product.

Tips

✓ *Tool 44: Sample Completed Frame.* This frame shows an example of how the Bordering on Excellence tool may be used.

✓ *Tool 45: Bordering on Excellence Frames.* This tool is a blank frame that provides an alternative format for analyzing either the needs of specific students or evaluating the obstacles inherent in a lesson. It is useful for training and teacher/parent conferences. Examples are provided for you to follow, along with blank frames for each of the four trouble areas faced by smart kids with learning difficulties. These frames can also be used to evaluate instructional materials, including curricular guides, books, teacher-made study guides, and workbooks (Iseman, Silverman, & Jeweler, 2010; Weinfeld et al., 2006).

Tool 44: Sample Completed Frame

Adaptations/Accommodations
Writing

Possible Stumbling Blocks

- ✓ the physical act of putting words on paper
- ✓ handwriting
- ✓ generating topics
- ✓ formulating topic sentences

- ✓ combining words into meaningful sentences
- ✓ using language mechanics effectively (e.g., grammar, punctuation, spelling)

- ✓ organizing sentences and incorporating adequate details and support statements into organized paragraphs
- ✓ revising and editing

Instructional Materials

- ✓ step-by-step written directions
- ✓ a proofreading checklist
- ✓ scoring rubrics, models, and anchor papers for students to evaluate their own work
- ✓ graphic organizers
- ✓ guides such as story starters, webs, story charts, outlines
- ✓ dictionaries, word banks, and thesauri
- ✓ personal dictionaries of misused and misspelled words
- ✓ highlighter to indicate errors/corrections
- ✓ copy of teacher notes or of another student's notes (NCR paper)
- ✓ pencil grips
- ✓ paper with raised lines
- ✓ mechanical pencils
- ✓ slant board

NOTES:

– 5 students with difficulties in writing

– written production required
- • literature webs (2 chapters)
- • vocabulary webs (2 words)
- • change matrix with specific evidence
- • written reflections

– I will need to address the following:
- • stumbling blocks (circled)
- • interventions (circled)
- • technology (circled)

– make sure students have access to computers/ software

– concerned with Johnny
- • great ideas, but poor production
- • doesn't have good computer skills
- • needs to be able to dictate ideas on tape or to an adult for transcription
- • needs to be able to use computer with word-predictive software

Teaching/ Assessment Methods

- ✓ focus on content rather than mechanics
- ✓ focus on quality rather than quantity
- ✓ begin with storyboards, guided imagery, dramatization, or projects before the writing process
- ✓ set important purposes for writing, such as writing for publication, writing to an expert, or writing to a famous person
- ✓ allow students to write in area of interest or expertise
- ✓ allow students to demonstrate understanding through alternative methods/products
- ✓ reduce or alter written requirements
- ✓ break down assignments into smaller, manageable parts
- ✓ additional time
- ✓ work with partners or small groups to confer for revising, editing, and proofreading

Assistive Technology

- ✓ voice recognition software
- ✓ organizational software
- ✓ electronic spellers and dictionaries
- ✓ tape recorder for student dictation and then transcription

- ✓ computer word processor with spelling and grammar checker or talking word processor
- ✓ portable keyboards
- ✓ word prediction software

- ✓ programs that allow writing to be read aloud
- ✓ programs that provide for audio spell checker, word prediction, and homophone distinction

Tool 45: Bordering on Excellence Frames

Adaptations/Accommodations
Writing

Possible Stumbling Blocks

- ✓ the physical act of putting words on paper
- ✓ handwriting
- ✓ generating topics
- ✓ formulating topic sentences

- ✓ combining words into meaningful sentences
- ✓ using language mechanics effectively (e.g., grammar, punctuation, spelling)

- ✓ organizing sentences and incorporating adequate details and support statements into organized paragraphs
- ✓ revising and editing

Instructional Materials	NOTES:	Teaching/ Assessment Methods
✓ step-by-step written directions ✓ a proofreading checklist ✓ scoring rubrics, models, and anchor papers for students to evaluate their own work ✓ graphic organizers ✓ guides such as story starters, webs, story charts, outlines ✓ dictionaries, word banks, and thesauri ✓ personal dictionaries of misused and misspelled words ✓ highlighter to indicate errors/corrections ✓ copy of teacher notes or of another student's notes (NCR paper) ✓ pencil grips ✓ paper with raised lines ✓ mechanical pencils ✓ slant board		✓ focus on content rather than mechanics ✓ focus on quality rather than quantity ✓ begin with storyboards, guided imagery, dramatization, or projects before the writing process ✓ set important purposes for writing, such as writing for publication, writing to an expert, or writing to a famous person ✓ allow students to write in area of interest or expertise ✓ allow students to demonstrate understanding through alternative methods/products ✓ reduce or alter written requirements ✓ break down assignments into smaller, manageable parts ✓ additional time ✓ work with partners or small groups to confer for revising, editing, and proofreading

Assistive Technology

- ✓ voice recognition software
- ✓ organizational software
- ✓ electronic spellers and dictionaries
- ✓ tape recorder for student dictation and then transcription

- ✓ computer word processor with spelling and grammar checker or talking word processor
- ✓ portable keyboards
- ✓ word prediction software

- ✓ programs that allow writing to be read aloud
- ✓ programs that provide for audio spell checker, word prediction, and homophone distinction

Tools 44 and 45: Bordering on Excellence Tools

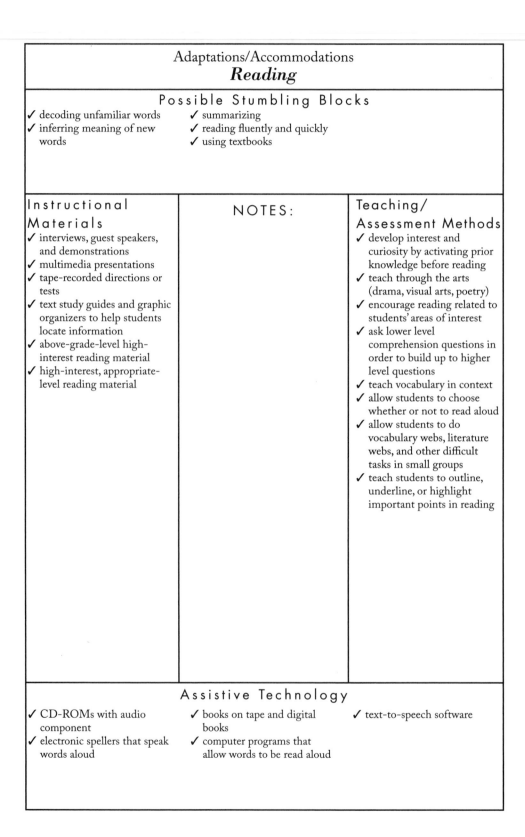

Adaptations/Accommodations
Reading

Possible Stumbling Blocks

✓ decoding unfamiliar words
✓ inferring meaning of new words
✓ summarizing
✓ reading fluently and quickly
✓ using textbooks

Instructional Materials

✓ interviews, guest speakers, and demonstrations
✓ multimedia presentations
✓ tape-recorded directions or tests
✓ text study guides and graphic organizers to help students locate information
✓ above-grade-level high-interest reading material
✓ high-interest, appropriate-level reading material

NOTES:

Teaching/ Assessment Methods

✓ develop interest and curiosity by activating prior knowledge before reading
✓ teach through the arts (drama, visual arts, poetry)
✓ encourage reading related to students' areas of interest
✓ ask lower level comprehension questions in order to build up to higher level questions
✓ teach vocabulary in context
✓ allow students to choose whether or not to read aloud
✓ allow students to do vocabulary webs, literature webs, and other difficult tasks in small groups
✓ teach students to outline, underline, or highlight important points in reading

Assistive Technology

✓ CD-ROMs with audio component
✓ electronic spellers that speak words aloud
✓ books on tape and digital books
✓ computer programs that allow words to be read aloud
✓ text-to-speech software

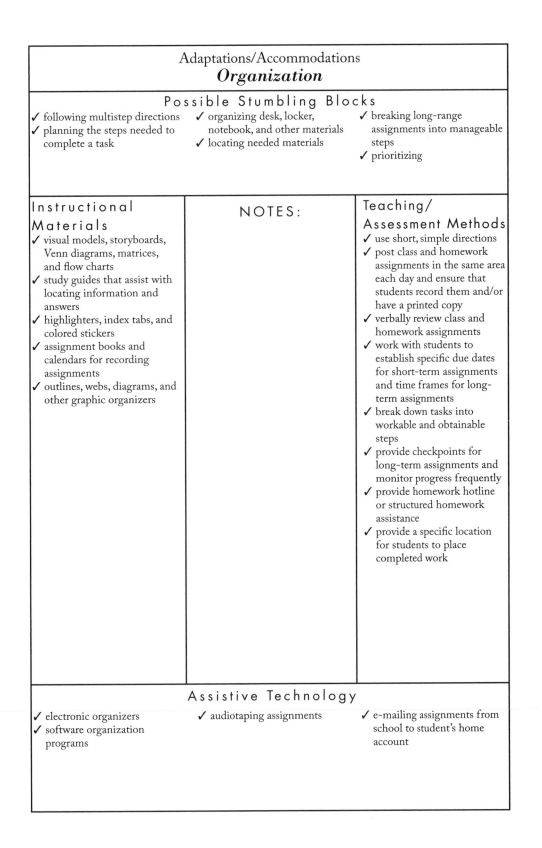

Adaptations/Accommodations
Organization

Possible Stumbling Blocks

- ✓ following multistep directions
- ✓ planning the steps needed to complete a task
- ✓ organizing desk, locker, notebook, and other materials
- ✓ locating needed materials
- ✓ breaking long-range assignments into manageable steps
- ✓ prioritizing

Instructional Materials

- ✓ visual models, storyboards, Venn diagrams, matrices, and flow charts
- ✓ study guides that assist with locating information and answers
- ✓ highlighters, index tabs, and colored stickers
- ✓ assignment books and calendars for recording assignments
- ✓ outlines, webs, diagrams, and other graphic organizers

NOTES:

Teaching/ Assessment Methods

- ✓ use short, simple directions
- ✓ post class and homework assignments in the same area each day and ensure that students record them and/or have a printed copy
- ✓ verbally review class and homework assignments
- ✓ work with students to establish specific due dates for short-term assignments and time frames for long-term assignments
- ✓ break down tasks into workable and obtainable steps
- ✓ provide checkpoints for long-term assignments and monitor progress frequently
- ✓ provide homework hotline or structured homework assistance
- ✓ provide a specific location for students to place completed work

Assistive Technology

- ✓ electronic organizers
- ✓ software organization programs
- ✓ audiotaping assignments
- ✓ e-mailing assignments from school to student's home account

Tools 44 and 45: Bordering on Excellence Tools

Tools 44 and 45: Bordering on Excellence Tools

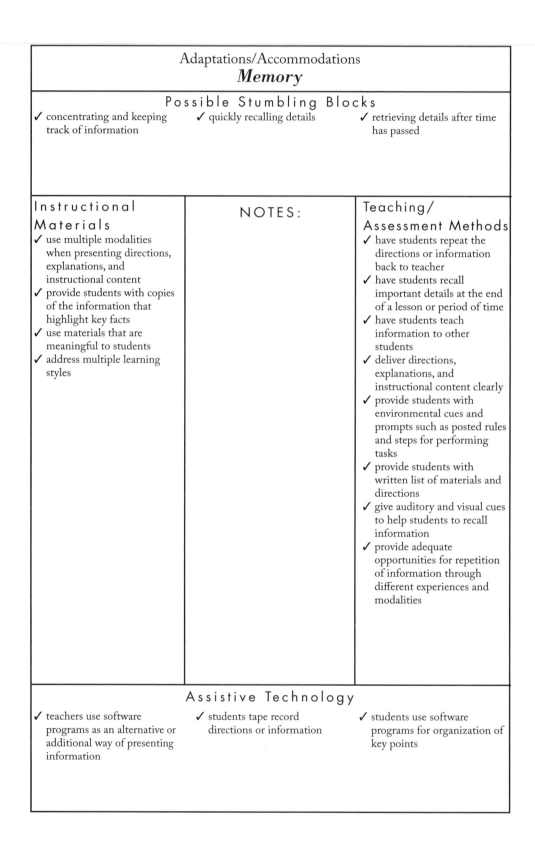

Adaptations/Accommodations
Memory

Possible Stumbling Blocks

✓ concentrating and keeping track of information

✓ quickly recalling details

✓ retrieving details after time has passed

Instructional Materials

✓ use multiple modalities when presenting directions, explanations, and instructional content
✓ provide students with copies of the information that highlight key facts
✓ use materials that are meaningful to students
✓ address multiple learning styles

NOTES:

Teaching/ Assessment Methods

✓ have students repeat the directions or information back to teacher
✓ have students recall important details at the end of a lesson or period of time
✓ have students teach information to other students
✓ deliver directions, explanations, and instructional content clearly
✓ provide students with environmental cues and prompts such as posted rules and steps for performing tasks
✓ provide students with written list of materials and directions
✓ give auditory and visual cues to help students to recall information
✓ provide adequate opportunities for repetition of information through different experiences and modalities

Assistive Technology

✓ teachers use software programs as an alternative or additional way of presenting information

✓ students tape record directions or information

✓ students use software programs for organization of key points

Tools 46–50:
The Team Approach

A bright student who has learning difficulties will experience greater success when involved adults and the student come together as a team. The tools that follow are designed to provide you with an effective way to bring a team together while building critical relationships with your student, the school staff, and her parents.

Tips

✓ *Tool 46: Conference Capture Sheet: Accommodations.* Use this tool with your student as the two of you prepare for conferences with the rest of the team. Record accommodations that have been tried and were effective in helping the student be successful. Use Tools 40, 41, and 43 as resources for generating ideas.

✓ *Tool 47: Student Tool: This Is What I Need to Succeed!* The student should complete this sheet alone or with an adult to use in meetings with individual teachers.

✓ *Tool 48: Parent-Teacher Conference Guide.* Use as you plan for your parent-teacher conference. Send a copy home to parents to complete and bring with them to the conference.

✓ *Tool 49: Evaluation Rating Scale.* Teachers, parents, and students use this sheet to evaluate student progress.

✓ *Tool 50: Parent Partnership Piece: Who's Who: Roles and Responsibilities.* Provide to parents prior to the conference.

Tool 46: Conference Capture Sheet: Accommodations

When the focus is on what the student needs and not just a list of accommodations to check off, then it helps the student understand what it is about the disability and his or her needs that make the accommodation necessary. Use this sheet to prepare for discussions about accommodations that will be put into place for the student.

Student Name: _____

Date: _____

Areas of Need:

- _____

- _____

- _____

- _____

Accommodations to Address the Needs:

- _____

- _____

- _____

- _____

Tool 47: Student Tool
This Is What I Need To Succeed!

Teachers want to help you figure out what you need to be successful in school. You may have tried some things in class that worked for you, things that you and your teacher have listed in your toolbox. In the space below tell your team what you think is helpful, so they can make a plan for you! You can ask your teacher or parent to help you plan and record what you want to say. In the box are areas in which you might need a little help.

Reading	Planning Time
Writing	Homework
Organizing	Completing Work
Memorizing	

- _____
- _____
- _____
- _____
- _____
- _____
- _____
- _____

Tools 46–50: The Team Approach

Tool 48: Parent-Teacher Conference Guide

Effective and efficient parent-teacher conferences require planning. The following tool can be used to structure a meaningful conference. When time is at a premium, it is a useful instrument because it contains information about the "total child"—socially, emotionally, and intellectually. In addition, this guide can be shared with the student before the parent-teacher conference so that everyone is on the same page.

Student Name: _____

Grade: _____   Date: _____

Areas in which student shows strength, growth, or need
(S = strength; G = growth; N = need)

Intellectual	Social	Emotional	Work Habits
❑ initiative ❑ resourcefulness ❑ problem solving ❑ follow through on plans ❑ evaluates own work ❑ originality	❑ cooperation with teacher ❑ cooperation with other students ❑ self-reliant ❑ leadership among peers ❑ ability to follow ❑ ability to give and take ❑ appreciation of others ❑ contributes to group effort ❑ responsibility	❑ self-control ❑ speech and conduct ❑ respect for rights and property of others ❑ consideration toward others ❑ recognition of standards ❑ attentiveness	❑ prompt ❑ persistent ❑ completes tasks commensurate with ability ❑ follows directions ❑ considerate of others while they are working ❑ independent ❑ achievement in relation to child's ability ❑ achievement in relation to child's goal

Tool 49: Evaluation Rating Scale

Directions: Teachers, parents, and students may use the following rating scale as a tool in order to evaluate student progress. Come back to this chart periodically to note progress.

Rate each statement according to the following scale:

1 = Never   2 = Sometimes   3 = Often   4 = Always

Date	Date	Date	Date	Area
				Student works independently.
				Student shows motivation and tenacity when presented with activities commensurate with his or her ability.
				Student uses a variety of opportunities to show what he or she knows.
				Student is attentive.
				Student uses organizational skills.
				Student uses time management skills.
				Student uses technological tools.
				Student uses research skills.
				Student uses problem-solving skills.
				Student engages in activities that require more than just factual recall of information.
				Student uses a variety of materials and resources.
				Student makes connections in and across subject areas.
				Student seeks help when needed.
				Student functions well in a variety of working groups.
				Student shows consideration for others.

Tools 46–50: The Team Approach

Tool 50: Parent Partnership Piece
Who's Who: Roles and Responsibilities

Dear Parent,

Sometimes the school system can be a complicated place to navigate. Knowing the roles and responsibilities of staff in the school will help you know where to go, depending on where you are in the process of getting help for your child. Although systems and names of positions vary from one district to the next, this list (adapted from Montgomery County Public Schools, 2004) may help you know who's who.

- *Teacher Advisor/Case Manager:* Point of entry contact; monitors students' overall progress; contacts parents regularly about progress; administers triennial re-evaluations; develops IEPs; consults with classroom teachers; problem solves; and refers unresolved issues to appropriate staff. Your child's case manager is _____.
- *General Education Teachers:* Serve as masters of content; collaborate with special educators; instruct students in curriculum; and provide accommodations and modifications. Your child's general education teacher(s) is/are _____.
- *Special Education Teachers:* Ensure access to challenging and rigorous curriculum; work on relevant IEP goals; accommodate and modify lessons; individually plan for and evaluate student progress; and instruct students in strategies and skills necessary to access curriculum. Your child's special education teacher(s) is/are _____.
- *Related Service Providers (e.g., Speech Language Pathologists, Occupational Therapists):* Provide related services; administer evaluations; evaluate progress; develop IEPs; and support classroom teachers. Your child's related service provider(s) is/are _____.
- *Special Education Instructional Assistants/Paraeducators:* Support classroom instruction; provide accommodations and modifications for students; teach small-group lessons; and assist teachers in any way necessary to ensure a well-run classroom environment. Your child's instructional assistants(s)/paraeducator(s) is/are _____.
- *Grade Level Counselors:* Schedule and counsel all students and provide information on resources. Your child's counselor(s) is/are

_____.

- *Resource Teacher for Special Education:* Coordinates special education services and collaborates with administration, educators, parents, and students. The RTSE at our school is _____.
- *Administration (e.g., Principal, Vice Principal, Student Support Specialist, etc.):* Oversee schoolwide issues; monitor programs; provide instructional leadership; and serve as resources for coordinators and parents. The administrators at our school are _____.

Hopefully, this information will clarify the roles and responsibilities of many of the staff members that support your child at school. If you have any questions, don't hesitate to contact me.

Sincerely,

Tools 46–50: The Team Approach

Tools 51 and 52: Intervention Plans

When the student's profile and his current program are carefully analyzed, interventions are selected that will provide opportunities to develop gifts, remove obstacles, and strengthen areas of need. The tools that follow are designed to provide you with an effective way to develop a program for the student that meets all of his unique needs.

Tips

✓ *Tool 51: Intervention Plan.* Complete at the meeting with the team. Use to analyze what is currently in place for the student and to make a plan of what could be done.

✓ *Tool 52: Parent Partnership Piece: Preparing for Your School Meeting.* Parents should use this to analyze all aspects of what currently is in place for their child and to make a plan of what could be done.

Tool 51: Intervention Plan

Name: _____   Date: _____

School: _____

Evidence of Gifts

Test Scores: _____

Performance in School (When does the student show interest, perseverance, self-regulation, and outstanding achievement?): _____

_____

Performance at Home and in the Community: _____

_____

Evidence of Learning Difficulties

Test Scores: _____

Performance in School: _____

_____

Behavioral/Attention Problems

Performance in School: _____

_____

Performance at Home and in the Community: _____

_____

Current Program

Gifted Instruction: _____

Adaptations: _____

Accommodations: _____

Tools 51 and 52: Intervention Plans

Special Instruction: _____

Behavior/Attention Management (plans, medication): _____

Social-Emotional Supports: _____

Case Management (Home-school communication, communication among

staff): _____

Recommendations

Gifted Instruction: _____

Adaptations: _____

Accommodations: _____

Special Instruction: _____

Behavior/Attention Management: _____

Social-Emotional Supports: _____

Case Management: _____

Next Steps

_____

_____

_____

_____

_____

Tool 52: Parent Partnership Piece
Preparing for Your School Meeting

Dear Parent,

Bright students who have learning difficulties experience greater success when parents and educators come together to make recommendations. You will have the opportunity at your child's meeting to share your thoughts with the team, as you hold critical information that will help guide us as we develop strategies for supporting your child. Therefore, I am including some suggestions that may help you to be an active participant at the meeting.

- Be prepared to share about how your child learns and what your child needs. If you have obtained a private evaluation about your child, consider providing it to the team to read and review in advance.
- Be ready to talk about the accommodations and services you feel your child needs.
- Feel free to take your own notes, but we will provide you with written documentation of the decisions we make as a team. You might want to create a file with all of your child's report cards, reports from meetings, correspondences, and behavioral or disciplinary records.
- You might find it valuable to have someone else there who knows your child (e.g., your spouse, a relative, a friend of the family) to also share his or her perspective, clarify information, and take notes.
- We encourage you to ask questions to clarify anything or get more information.
- We will establish next steps and plans for ongoing communication. Please feel free to suggest what would best work for you so that we can keep you informed and involved.
- Prior to the meeting, contact me if you have any questions about the purpose of and the procedures for the meeting.

Sincerely,

Keeping the Bright Turned On!

❏ **Alternatives:** Provide lists of projects that students can use to show what they know instead of the ordinary written report. Give opportunities for them to choose these alternatives, so they can explore their strengths and build a repertoire of ways to demonstrate their understanding.

❏ **Time With Peers:** Students benefit from spending time with other students like them. Providing time for students to get together helps with self-awareness. Form a small group or groups of bright students with learning difficulties (mixed ages if necessary) to meet periodically to work together on projects or talk about common issues that they have. This could occur on a class level, as well as within a grade or school.

❏ **Mentoring:** Find an older student to mentor a younger student. This helps let the student know that he is not alone and also gives him a chance to make a friend.

❏ **Go for the Gold!** Have students decide on and set a goal for themselves. Have them break it down into smaller, measurable, and achievable steps. Then keep track of their progress in reaching their goals and the "gold."

chapter 4

How Do I Teach Them?

Instruction begins when you, the teacher, learn from the learner; put yourself in his place so that you may understand . . . what he learns and the way he understands it.

—Søren Kierkegaard

Guiding Questions

❑ What are effective instructional strategies and approaches that work for these students?

❑ How do I improve my students' reading, writing, and organization skills?

❑ How do I use information about my students' strengths and weaknesses to plan lessons and units that will meet their needs?

Word Sparks

✓ instructional strategies   ✓ what works
✓ skills   ✓ motivation
✓ challenge   ✓ writers
✓ choice   ✓ readers

Chapter Overview

A S an educator, you wear many hats, yet your primary role is to advance the learning process for your students. The ideas and tools in this chapter are research based, but they have also proven effective in real classrooms with twice-exceptional students. Although these approaches and techniques are effective for many different kinds of students and what works for twice-exceptional students often works for all students, bright students with learning difficulties cannot survive or thrive in a traditional learning environment that lacks the critical components described below.

Instructional Approaches That Work

Develop a Positive Relationship With the Student

In the right climate, where students know and feel they are respected and valued for their uniqueness, anything is possible. When students feel unsafe or when they perceive they are not valued or respected, the instruction and interventions, however appropriate, may fail. Many excellent teachers fail to make a connection with these students and wonder why the students are not responding to their efforts. These kids are often very good at picking up on subtle clues about how their teachers feel about them. They know when they are a burden on their teachers and when they have disappointed them. They know when an adult thinks they are lazy, whether those words are said aloud or not. They feel ignored when teachers do not ask them what they think or what they want. In these cases, they often respond by refusing or sabotaging their teacher's efforts at helping them. They may withdraw from the learning process, seeming more and more unmotivated and disengaged. They often pick up cues from body language and intonation, in addition to the words that are spoken. Students will respond positively to genuineness and authenticity, while rejecting interactions they experience or perceive as phony, uncaring, or disrespectful. It is not only critical what we do, but how we do it.

Teach and Develop Critical Thinking

The higher level thinking skills of creating, evaluating, and analyzing (Bloom's taxonomy) come naturally to these students, but will not be evident without opportunity and practice. Plan lessons that tap into these abilities and give students open-ended tasks that allow them to apply these strengths, and you will see the engagement and learning of these students skyrocket. They love a challenge! The more complex a task, the more energy they bring to it and the harder they will work at it. An experienced teacher explained it this way: "One way I often perked my students up was by saying, 'This is going to be really hard, but it's going to be really fun!'" The harder the question posed to them, the more enthusiastic the response. Ask them to solve a complex problem, defend an opinion, or respond to an interpretive question, and you will get a thoughtful, passionate response.

Conceptual Learning

Concepts allow students to mentally organize objects, events, or ideas based on common attributes (Bruner, 1967). These students respond best to instruction that is focused on concepts and principles rather than on details and rote learning. They do well when instruction begins with the big picture and allows them to connect their wealth of prior knowledge to new knowledge. Once the concept has been firmly attained, they are better able to retain facts and details that relate to the concept. This type of instruction can also be described as "whole-to-part" because instruction starts with the "whole" or big picture and works down to the "part" or details. These students already have much conceptual knowledge in their heads that teachers can link so that they don't have to explicitly teach ideas bit by bit.

Teach and Develop Creative Thinking

Ask a parent or teacher of a twice-exceptional student to pick five adjectives that describe the student, and a majority of the time, "creative" will be one of those adjectives. But creative thinking does not mean being artistic, nor is it synonymous with the arts, as not all students are strong in those areas. These students are naturally creative thinkers. They love to generate new ideas or to put a new spin on an old one. They like to come up with original ways to solve a problem or to develop a unique perspective. Tap into this ability and desire to create by using brainstorming techniques and by giving students open-ended tasks and problems that can be solved in many ways. These students often love creative writing assignments that allow them to use their imaginations and to play with words in unique ways.

Teach Thematically

These students learn best when there is an overarching theme or concept that connects the learning objectives amongst the disciplines. For example, students may be working on fractions in math, writing persuasively in English, learning about plants in science, and learning about migration in social studies. These topics may seem disconnected, and a twice-exceptional student may have trouble holding the different pieces in her memory and making sense of it all. Add in the theme of effects of global warming, study each of these topics from this angle, and the student's understanding, engagement, and enthusiasm will increase exponentially!

Integrate the Arts

Bright kids with learning difficulties often gravitate to or have a natural talent in the visual and/or performing arts. Many students who could not read or write could create a painting or deliver a monologue that would bring you to tears. Teach them about curriculum-relevant art and artists and allow them to demonstrate their knowledge by creating a painting, a sculpture, a dance, a song, or a skit, and you will see joyful learning at its best!

Teach Using Multiple Intelligences and Learning Styles Theories

Most educators are aware of these theories, but many do not incorporate them into instruction. Determine the MI strengths of your students and help them discover their learning style preferences. Then ensure that over a course of study, students have varied pathways for learning and demonstrating knowledge that use their strengths. Mix up your instruction so that students develop all of their intelligences and every student has an opportunity to shine.

Connect to Interests

Interest is a powerful motivator for twice-exceptional students. Students who appear unable to focus for more than 5 seconds at a time turn into focused individuals who do not want to stop working on a task. The difference is choice, self-selection, and carefully developed tasks that tap into a student's existing or possible interests. One teacher confessed that her students hated the novel she chose for their first unit and their performance that quarter was lackluster at best. The next quarter, she used information that reflected on their personal interests and selected three novels for the students to choose from that she felt they would really like. She said that they all read, participated, and submitted incredible projects. Although some will have restricted interests (like students with Asperger's syndrome), many bright students with learning difficulties have varied, existing interests and their curiosity is easily piqued. You can either connect the curriculum to their existing interests or develop their interest in an area connected to the curriculum. Either way, you will be able to ride the wave of interest far into the ocean of other activities and lessons that your students would otherwise find boring.

Utilize Instructional and Assistive Technology

Bright students with learning difficulties love technology! Many are naturally drawn to video games, computers, and the latest gadgets; they love to use them and think about how they work. Tap into this inherent interest by using technology in the classroom for instruction and teaching them how to use assistive technology (AT) designed to assist students with disabilities. Today's 21st-century teachers use a variety of technologies for instruction, such as PowerPoint-assisted lectures, streaming video clips, WebQuests, pictures from Google Images, Promethean Boards, and more. Struggling readers can use a variety of tools and software (e.g., MP3 players, Kurzweil

3000, Write:OutLoud, ReadPlease, WordQ) to listen to text that is above their reading level. Struggling writers benefit from software (e.g., Inspiration, WordQ, Clicker, Write:OutLoud, Draft:Builder, Dragon NaturallySpeaking, SpeakQ) to support their organizational, spelling, handwriting, and note-taking difficulties.

Provide Strategy and Metacognitive Instruction

Teaching students strategies allows them to internalize and generalize a learning process so that they learn not only content and information, but also how to be successful, independent learners. A well-practiced strategy is a tool that is always in the student's toolkit and one he can pull out and use when needed. An example of a strategy that works for these kids is the University of Kansas' Center for Research on Learning's Theme Writing Strategy, which uses TOWER (Think, Organize, Write, Evaluate, Refine) to help students break down and recreate the writing process when given a new writing task (see http://www.ku-crl.org/sim/strategies.shtml for this strategy and others developed by the University of Kansas). Metacognitive instruction means teaching students to be reflective and to be able to think about their thinking, and thus improve their learning process. Asking them what they did well and how it could be improved helps build this type of thinking. Giving them specific feedback regarding their learning behaviors and modeling metacognitive thinking (think-alouds) teaches them how to actively engage in a productive learning and thinking process and then how to reflect upon and self-evaluate their own performance.

Emphasize Project-Based Learning

These students thrive in classrooms where long-term, student-driven projects abound. You will be amazed at how committed to an independent or group project students can be when they are able to select and develop their topic, chart a course for learning about this topic using various resources, and determine the type of product that will showcase their acquired knowledge. Twice-exceptional students also love a tough problem and problem-based learning that allows them to tackle a real-world, authentic issue (such as a community issue from a local paper). They typically prefer active learning that allows them to do something, rather than passively receiving information. Long-term projects allow them to apply their learning in a way that connects all of the lessons, activities, and assessments that go on in their day-to-day classes. Projects help them see how the concepts, facts, and skills within the unit relate to the big picture and to themselves. Students often forget information learned in a course but generally remember their big projects because the learning was personal and purposeful. Projects are enjoyable for these students because they generally culminate in a creative product that serves as evidence of the learning that occurred along the way.

Encourage Cooperative, Interactive Learning

These kids benefit from interactive learning tasks that allow them to be actively involved with their peers. When given a role or job that allows them to use their strengths (such as the reporter instead of the recorder), they often enjoy working with other students to accomplish group tasks and can contribute a great deal. Opportunities for interactive learning via shared inquiry, structured discussions, student-to-student discourse, think-pair-share, jigsaws, role-play, simulations, and more should be plentiful.

Multisensory Instruction

Paper-and-pencil tasks often are difficult for kids with learning difficulties. They learn best from instruction that allows them to use all of their senses to build understanding of a concept. This means not just reading and writing about a topic but hearing, saying, seeing, touching, and smelling it. A day in a classroom where the teacher emphasizes multisensory instruction might have the students using manipulatives to learn and practice a new math concept, viewing and then discussing a social studies video, handling materials and making observations during a science lab experiment, writing and illustrating a poem and then reading and listening to classmates' poems, and interpreting and performing a scene from a play. These students are more likely to retain information when all of their senses are involved during the learning process. Field trips and experiential/hands-on tasks are a great way to get these kids out into the world looking, touching, smelling, hearing, and learning with all of their senses.

Utilize Differentiation Strategies

Gifted students (with and without disabilities) consistently require instruction above and beyond the regular curriculum. Some districts provide pull-out or self-contained gifted programs, but most often, gifted students who learn differently are in large, general education classrooms. Your classroom is likely such a class, so you must be able to use flexible grouping and to adjust instruction based on student readiness, interest, and learning style (see Tomlinson, 2000, for more on differentiation). Differentiated instructional strategies, such as compacting, acceleration, learning centers, anchor activities, independent study, and tiered lessons and assessments, allow you to challenge your students when they are ready for it.

Teaching Skills

As you know, the most important thing for a teacher to do for these kids is to teach to their strengths and to nurture their gifts and talents in the ways described above. But it is also critical to teach these students how to be better readers, stronger writers, and independent learners. If you take an approach that only focuses on the weaknesses, you are very likely to find these students resistant. Recommendations are provided below for effectively addressing weaknesses in core academic areas. Hook the students into their learning tasks (see Tool 56) and they will want to read and write. When they want to engage in lessons and tasks, their learning of skills is maximized. Implementing research-based methods for improving their skills will then be sure to have a positive effect and progress will be visible.

Reading

Bright students with reading problems typically have excellent listening comprehension, oral expression, vocabulary, and background knowledge that help them to compensate for their difficulties. They typically have weaknesses in phonemic awareness, decoding, and reading fluency that interfere with their ability to construct meaning from text independently. These students require a reading decoding program that: (a) is structured and systematic (has a scope and sequence), (b) is rule-based and teaches syllable types and syllable division, (c) is multisensory, (d) has a phonemic awareness component, and (e) incorporates encoding/spelling instruction. The Wilson Reading Program has proven successful with remediating reading problems. Other programs and materials that target decoding, encoding, and fluency can also be effective.

Writing

Why is writing so hard for these kids? Many bright students with learning difficulties will be good at every other academic subject, including reading, and yet struggle significantly with representing their thoughts on paper. Writing is such a complex skill because it requires a student to have (at minimum) good fine motor control, spelling ability, vocabulary, memory, and organization. To get an idea of how frustrating and challenging writing can be for some of these students, write for 2 minutes using your nondominant hand (see Tool 54).

These kids also have a lot of strengths that they bring to the table. They have great imaginations and are very creative. They have large vocabularies and can be uniquely expressive with words. They have a lot of ideas swimming around in their heads just waiting to get out, and because these students do want to communicate their ideas, there are ways to motivate and entice them to write. Once they desire to write and are producing writing, the teacher can weave in mini-lessons regarding the writing process, writing strategies (e.g., TOWER, brainstorming, graphic organizers), use of assistive technology, and writing skills (e.g., the 6+1 Traits of Writing). Then, give them lots of practice with fun writing prompts (see Tool 62) and watch them develop into authors.

Organization

One of the biggest challenges that these students, their teachers, and their parents face is supporting their executive functioning deficits. Although not all of them face organizational pitfalls, most of them do on a daily basis and it is often a primary reason for lack of academic success in a traditional school setting. Typical concerns are task initiation, remaining on task, shifting between tasks, managing time wisely, and organization of materials and space. Many students have binders that are exploding and papers that disappear into black holes. Others may look organized but have no idea how to manage their workload. Many of these kids are also resistant to organizational support. They feel they have a system that "works" for them (even when it clearly isn't working) and don't want to abide by your organization rules. They may resist using a daily homework planner by saying they "know" what their homework is. They may refuse to organize their desk or binder by saying, "I like it that way!"

How do we help them learn to be organized? These students need an approach that involves coaching and support of organization skills (see Tool 65). They generally respond well when provided with options and allowed to choose a system, try it out, and determine how and if it needs to be tweaked.

Student Profiles

Sarah

Sarah's teachers use a variety of instructional approaches and strategies that are aligned with her strengths. Because she is so verbal, they utilize a lot of discussion strategies such as think-pair-share, Socratic seminars, and fishbowls. They emphasize a project-based approach over lots of little daily assignments and provide her with many choices so that she is able to develop interest areas through these long-term tasks. Her teacher compacts instruction for Sarah and other advanced students in the class, which then buys them time to work at interest and enrichment centers and on highly structured yet independent research projects.

Jeremy

Jeremy's teachers have taken the time to develop a strong relationship with him and to really get to know him. They talk with him about topics of interest and share with him things about which they are currently reading and learning. They bring him articles from the newspaper and nonfiction books from their personal libraries that he might find of interest. They have administered general and curriculum-specific interest inventories, learning style inventories, and multiple intelligences inventories to help determine his tendencies as a learner and his preferences. His teachers look ahead at each instructional unit and plan for connections to Jeremy's interests to increase his engagement with the curriculum. They utilize a lot of instructional technology in the form of PowerPoint-assisted lectures, streaming video and DVDs, and podcasts. Jeremy has been trained in the use of Inspiration and voice recognition software so that when it is time for him to write, he develops his own graphic organizer and then dictates his response to the computer.

Darryl

Darryl's reading/writing, math, and science/social studies teachers plan collaboratively to design their units around a common theme. They have used themes based on their own areas of expertise and interest from real-world social studies and science happenings (e.g., disasters, current events, discoveries), and have at times utilized commercial thematic units (e.g., Interact simulations) to connect their disciplines and lessons over time. All students, including Darryl, are incredibly engaged, activating prior knowledge and learning the curriculum objectives under the bigger umbrella of the theme. The teachers planned ahead and designed lessons that are multisensory and created product choices to ensure that students with different strengths can find a way to show what they know. Darryl frequently chooses to create visual-spatial representations of his knowledge but has been known to choose a poetry or computer-based product that highlights his verbal strengths as well.

Conclusion

Now that you have an understanding of what it takes to implement appropriate instruction that is aligned with the strengths of your students, you are ready to engage with the tools we've created. Flexibility is the key. Provide lots of alternatives and options and just enough structure and adult support so that your students will be as successful and independent as possible. These tools will support your work with bright students with learning difficulties as you strive to provide instruction that is sensitive and responsive to their strengths and weaknesses.

Tools 53 and 54: Connecting With Students

You must develop a trusting, comfortable relationship with these students if you hope to make a difference academically. These tools will help you connect and empathize with the smart kids with learning difficulties in your classroom.

Tips

✓ *Tool 53: Relationship Building Checklist.* Use these ideas to develop a positive relationship with your students. It will pay off and they will see you as a partner, not an adversary. Academic growth will not only be possible, but visible and enjoyable!

✓ *Tool 54: In Their Shoes.* This tool can be used to develop empathy with struggling students. Experiencing what your students experience is important, yet feeling what they feel is critical. They must believe you have experienced *and* felt what they have for there to be true empathy. The most effective way to use this tool is in a group setting so that participants feel like a student in a classroom. The leader of the activity reads the question to the group and asks them to write at least three complete sentences using their best handwriting and spelling/punctuation. Because this is a timed activity, they are not to start until you tell them to. Just before having them begin, tell them to switch their pens/pencils to their nondominant hand and then start the timer. After the 2 minutes are up, debrief the activity using the questions on this tool.

Tool 53:
Relationship Building Checklist

Directions: Mark each item below in the following way: A = I already do that! or W = I will do that!

_____ Reach out to the students on a personal level. Know them well and discover their interests. Connect over things you share in common. Engage them in conversations about their thoughts, their lives, their experiences, and their feelings. Many of these students have very active mental lives or interesting activities they engage in outside of school.
Questions to ask:
❏ What do you do when you have free time?
❏ When are you the happiest? What makes you smile?
❏ What do you think about?

_____ Show the students that you like them. These kids often perceive that their teachers don't like or appreciate them. They receive negative attention from teachers because they need so much help, because they often blurt out off-topic ideas before being called on, or because they never get their work done. When they feel they are not liked, they tend to shut down.
Things to do:
❏ Smile at the student. A little smile goes a long way!
❏ Ask about your student's day/weekend and laugh at his jokes or stories.
❏ Praise her for doing the right thing, even if it's simply what is expected.
❏ Mirror his strengths back to him by vocalizing what you see (e.g., "I like how specific your word choice is, Jeremy!").
❏ Call on the student and use her name during instruction. Ask her to be the expert on topics related to her passion areas.

_____ Encourage and acknowledge risk taking and set the expectation with all students that it is better to try and fail then never to try at all. Prevent unhealthy competition among your students by teaching them that differences are normal, people have strengths in different areas, and that our weaknesses do not define us.
Things to say:
❏ I know you can do it. I will help you.
❏ You are working really hard. I appreciate your effort!

❑   Even if you don't know the answer, give it a try!

❑   That came really easily to you . . . let's look for a new challenge.

_____   Be real and human to your students. Tell them about yourself, your life, your strengths, interests, and most importantly, your weaknesses. If they know more than you do about a topic, let them teach you. Let them see your imperfections, and they will be more likely to trust you with their own.

Things to say:

❑   This is what I like/don't like (am good/bad at) . . .

❑   I don't know the answer to that. Do you? How can we figure it out?

❑   Oops! I made a mistake. Oh well, nobody is perfect! What can I do to fix it?

Tools 53 and 54: Connecting With Students

Tool 54: In Their Shoes

Directions: Set a timer for 2 minutes and try to write at least *three good, complete sentences* in response to the question below using your *nondominant hand*. So, if you are a "righty," write with your left hand. Try to make the writing neat and legible and to communicate your ideas to the best of your ability.

Based on your understanding of the characteristics of bright students with learning difficulties, what are some possible reasons that many of these students display lack of motivation for many school tasks?

_____

_____

_____

_____

_____

_____

Reflection Questions:

1. How did writing with your nondominant hand affect your writing (e.g., quantity, quality, spelling, mechanics, handwriting) and your thinking?
2. What emotions did you feel during this task?
3. Would you want to share this writing with your peers? Why or why not?
4. Do you have students whose writing looks like this?
5. If you had to do this five more times today, what would be your reaction?
6. Why is it important to provide accommodations and alternatives to writing for bright students with writing difficulties? Is writing a valid assessment of content knowledge for these students?

Tools 55–58:
Aligning Instruction
With Strengths

One of the most important things to remember when teaching bright students with learning difficulties is to teach to their strengths. In order to do this, you must first be able to identify those strengths. The next step is to be aware of pedagogy and teaching strategies that will allow you to capitalize on and nurture the strengths of your students. Aligning instruction to the students' strengths involves more than just placing them in the higher math or reading group. It requires tailoring the instructional approach based on the way they learn best. The tools in this section will support you to utilize research-based instructional strategies and approaches for these students that are proven to work.

Tips

- ✓ *Tool 55: If . . . Then . . .* This chart will help you identify strengths within the student and select instructional approaches and strategies that will work for that student. More information about each strategy can be found in Tool 58.
- ✓ *Tool 56: The Hooks.* This mini-poster can be hung by your desk as a quick reference during lesson planning or to evaluate the quality of a lesson or unit.
- ✓ *Tool 57: What Works!* This tool is based on years of research and classroom application with gifted students with learning disabilities (Montgomery County Public Schools, 2004; Weinfeld et al., 2006). The strategies and methods on the chart were developed with the strengths and weaknesses of GT/LD students in mind (students like Darryl). This section encompasses social-emotional and academic recommendations including specific strategies for each content area. What works best for these students is an interdisciplinary approach that integrates thinking and learning skills and unifies content and process. Students learn best when provided with information in a variety of ways.
- ✓ *Tool 58: Instructional Strategies That Work!* This list of instructional strategies is for use during lesson planning. All have been chosen for this list based on successful implementation with twice-exceptional students and alignment with the research-based best practices found in the What Works! chart.

Tool 55: If . . . Then . . .

Student Name: _____

If the Student Has Strong . . .	Then Teachers Should . . .	Possible Strategies
• Verbal skills/ vocabulary	• Emphasize discussion, discourse, questioning, and oral presentations. • Pair visual information with verbal information.	• Paired verbal fluency • Shared inquiry discussions
• Visual-spatial skills	• Incorporate visuals, hands-on experiences, and visual imagery. • Start with the big picture before introducing details. • Pair verbal information with visual support.	• Visualization (guided imagery) • Picture interpretation
• Interpersonal skills	• Emphasize cooperative learning and group tasks. • Provide leadership opportunities. • Encourage student discourse.	• Jigsaws • Expert groups
• Problem-solving and reasoning skills	• Provide tasks that are open-ended or questions that have many possible answers. • Teach thinking and reasoning skills.	• de Bono's Six Hats • Paul's Reasoning Wheel
• Acquisition of concepts	• Compact instruction. • Emphasize concepts over details/facts. • Teach through discovery. • Emphasize projects.	• Guess box • Independent study
• Ability to make connections	• Teach thematically and connect the disciplines. • Connect new information to prior knowledge	• K-W-L charts • Concept maps

• Critical thinking skills	• Provide rigorous content and tasks that require higher level thinking (analysis, evaluation, synthesis). • Teach students how to think. • Emphasize strategies and metacognitive thinking.	• Bloom's taxonomy • Synectics • The Important Thing
• Curiosity	• Provide enrichment. • Emphasize project-based learning. • Encourage student questions. • Incorporate novelty. • Nurture and develop interests.	• Question cubes • Inquiry/research projects
• Specific talents and interests	• Allow varied products and demonstrations of mastery based on student's strengths, talents, or interests. • Provide choices.	• Interest inventory • Product preferences (Tool 9)
• Creativity	• Integrate visual and performing arts. • Provide opportunities for creative writing. • Support generation of original and varied ideas. • Have students develop projects that allow them to utilize their learning styles and MI strengths.	• Entry and exit points • Open-ended assignments

Tools 55–58: Aligning Instruction With Strengths

Tool 56: The Hooks

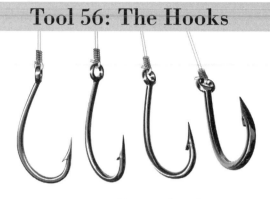

The following are components of instruction that are sure to engage your students!

Critical Thinking

✓ Develop lessons and assignments that require higher level thinking skills such as analysis, synthesis, evaluation, and reasoning.
✓ Ask students to think about their thinking (metacognition).
✓ Take students beyond knowledge to application of knowledge.

Complexity/Challenge

✓ These kids love a challenge! Make it harder and they'll work harder. But remember, challenge does not mean "more" work.
✓ Appropriately differentiate content to provide "just right" instruction.
✓ Emphasize depth vs. breadth.

Creativity

✓ Create open-ended problems for students to solve.
✓ Require products that allow students to demonstrate originality.
✓ Include creative writing as part of instruction.
✓ Infuse the visual and performing arts into content instruction and assessment.

Context

✓ Present the "big picture" before a new unit of study.
✓ Use overarching themes to connect disciplines and topics.
✓ Create or elicit real-world applications and personal connections.
✓ Make content "real" by providing hands-on learning opportunities.
✓ Use a lot of visuals and multimedia resources to create context for new content.

Choice

✓ Provide options periodically that are based on various learning styles and multiple intelligences.
✓ Provide options that are based on student interests and passions.
✓ Allow a student to approach an assignment from a unique angle or perspective.

Compensatory Tools and Strategies

✓ Don't let the disability get in the way of the above components. Use computers, recorded books, assistive technology, and instructional strategies to support students as they strive to demonstrate the full extent of their knowledge.

Tools 55–58: Aligning Instruction With Strengths

Tool 57: What Works!

Directions: Review each area of the chart (as is relevant to your position) and rate your use of each component. Periodically come back to this and use a different colored pen to indicate where you are at that time. This way your progress will be visible!

Key: 1 = I'm just beginning, 3 = I'm halfway there, 5 = I got it!

Climate	
1 2 3 4 5	Supports an understanding of students' unique strengths and needs
1 2 3 4 5	Promotes self-advocacy skills
1 2 3 4 5	Is a comfortable, yet challenging, classroom where there is a stimulating environment (e.g., posters, collections, products)
1 2 3 4 5	Has highly visible class standards and expectations for performance for both students and the teacher
1 2 3 4 5	Supports student freedom of movement within the classroom
1 2 3 4 5	Includes interactive participation
1 2 3 4 5	Has flexibility (i.e., able to adjust lessons and expectations based on student needs)
1 2 3 4 5	Has high standards
1 2 3 4 5	Uses cooperative groups
1 2 3 4 5	Includes individualized programming
1 2 3 4 5	Has instruction on active listening
1 2 3 4 5	Has instruction on conflict resolution
1 2 3 4 5	Provides multimedia resources (e.g., computer, DVDs, tape recorders)
1 2 3 4 5	Provides technological tools (e.g., word processors, calculators, spell checkers)

Social-Emotional	
1 2 3 4 5	Respects students
1 2 3 4 5	Encourages students
1 2 3 4 5	Connects to students through strengths/interests
1 2 3 4 5	Focuses on strengths, analyzes successes, and applies strengths to areas of weakness
1 2 3 4 5	Teaches conflict resolution skills
1 2 3 4 5	Teaches self-efficacy

1 2 3 4 5	Teaches self-advocacy
1 2 3 4 5	Offers choices
1 2 3 4 5	Offers alternative ideas and options
1 2 3 4 5	Provides extracurricular enrichment activities
1 2 3 4 5	Teaches students to channel frustrations
1 2 3 4 5	Eases and removes barriers and plans for the future
1 2 3 4 5	Uses nonverbal strategies to support students
1 2 3 4 5	Uses discipline as a "teachable moment"
1 2 3 4 5	Has open lines of communication
1 2 3 4 5	Encourages risk taking
1 2 3 4 5	Offers opportunities to practice skills to build confidence

Gifted Instruction	
1 2 3 4 5	Includes models for gifted education (e.g., multiple intelligences, Creative Problem Solving, Bloom's taxonomy)
1 2 3 4 5	Has activities that focus on students' gifts and interests
1 2 3 4 5	Offers open-ended outlets for the demonstration of knowledge
1 2 3 4 5	Differentiates instruction
1 2 3 4 5	Provides tasks that fit students' learning styles
1 2 3 4 5	Includes multisensory instruction
1 2 3 4 5	Supports guided discovery (K-W-L organizers), especially when introducing new topics
1 2 3 4 5	Provides support and clarification for embedded directions, both oral and written
1 2 3 4 5	Offers students choices
1 2 3 4 5	Gives alternative product options
1 2 3 4 5	Allows for collaboratively designed rubrics
1 2 3 4 5	Provides hands-on experiences
1 2 3 4 5	Gives real-life tasks
1 2 3 4 5	Integrates visual and performing arts

Thinking	
1 2 3 4 5	Teaches thinking strategies
1 2 3 4 5	Models thinking strategies
1 2 3 4 5	Practices thinking strategies in the classroom
1 2 3 4 5	Applies thinking strategies

Tools 55–58: Aligning Instruction With Strengths

1 2 3 4 5	Helps students to formulate questions; think through logic problems; use the Socratic method; require active participation in the learning process; apply abstract concepts to everyday occurrences; use think-alouds to model the thinking process; develop a thinking language; and search for their own solutions
1 2 3 4 5	Utilizes metacognitive skills
1 2 3 4 5	Transfers/applies thinking strategies that work in areas of strength to areas of need

Reading	
1 2 3 4 5	Emphasizes comprehension, listening, and gaining information
1 2 3 4 5	Uses literature for stimulating reading interest
1 2 3 4 5	Includes high-interest, personal reading material that may be above grade level
1 2 3 4 5	Provides programs like Junior Great Books that build abstract reasoning and comprehension skills
1 2 3 4 5	Develops expository reading
1 2 3 4 5	Offers oral discussion using supporting text
1 2 3 4 5	Gives explicit instruction in phonological awareness, phonics, and decoding (e.g., Wilson Reading Program)
1 2 3 4 5	Includes accommodations like books on tape and text-to-speech software

Writing	
1 2 3 4 5	Establishes the writing process through ongoing discussion and practice
1 2 3 4 5	Provides assistive technology (e.g., portable word processors, computers, electronic spellers, organizational software, word-predictive software)
1 2 3 4 5	Gives students graphic organizers
1 2 3 4 5	Teaches mind-mapping strategies
1 2 3 4 5	Offers extended time for completion of work
1 2 3 4 5	Provides clearly written expectations for writing tasks
1 2 3 4 5	Includes writing prompts
1 2 3 4 5	Gives students rubrics
1 2 3 4 5	Teaches proofreading for one type of error at a time
1 2 3 4 5	Gives students highlighters to indicate corrections
1 2 3 4 5	Supports publication or writing for an audience

Tools 55–58: Aligning Instruction With Strengths

	Organization
1 2 3 4 5	Provides electronic organizers
1 2 3 4 5	Offers software organization programs
1 2 3 4 5	Gives students study guides that assist with locating information and answers
1 2 3 4 5	Uses assignment books and calendars for recording assignments
1 2 3 4 5	Gives students graphic organizers (e.g., outlines, webs, diagrams, storyboards, flow charts)
1 2 3 4 5	Works with students to establish specific due dates for short assignments and time frames for long-term assignments
1 2 3 4 5	Breaks up tasks into workable and obtainable steps
1 2 3 4 5	Provides checkpoints for long-term assignments and monitoring progress frequently
1 2 3 4 5	Allows time to organize materials and assignments
1 2 3 4 5	Provides a homework hotline or web page
1 2 3 4 5	Provides a specific location for students to place completed work
1 2 3 4 5	Monitors students' accuracy in recording assignments and/or providing printed copy

	Memory
1 2 3 4 5	Uses multiple modalities, including art and simulations, when presenting directions, explanations, and instructional content
1 2 3 4 5	Utilizes a multiple intelligences approach
1 2 3 4 5	Provides students with a copy of the information that highlights key facts
1 2 3 4 5	Has students sequence activities after a lesson or event
1 2 3 4 5	Has students serve as experts on a topic
1 2 3 4 5	Has students tape record directions or information
1 2 3 4 5	Provides students with environmental cues and prompts (e.g., posted rules, steps for performing tasks)
1 2 3 4 5	Allows students to use resources in the environment to recall information (e.g., notes, textbooks, pictures)
1 2 3 4 5	Relates information presented to students' previous experiences
1 2 3 4 5	Has students outline, highlight, underline, or summarize information that should be remembered

1 2 3 4 5	Tells students what to listen for when being given directions or receiving information
1 2 3 4 5	Gives students associative cues or mnemonic devices
1 2 3 4 5	Teaches visual imagery

Handwriting	
1 2 3 4 5	Focuses on form
1 2 3 4 5	Provides mechanical pencils and grips
1 2 3 4 5	Teaches an appropriate handwriting program (e.g., Handwriting Without Tears)
1 2 3 4 5	Offers assistive technology tools

Mathematics	
1 2 3 4 5	Preassesses students' mastery of mathematical categories (e.g., decimals, fractions, whole numbers, probability)
1 2 3 4 5	Preassesses students' mastery of mathematical objectives
1 2 3 4 5	Focuses on developing conceptual skills and problem-solving strategies
1 2 3 4 5	Includes a multidisciplinary approach
1 2 3 4 5	Includes an interactive approach
1 2 3 4 5	Gives hands-on tasks
1 2 3 4 5	Uses manipulatives
1 2 3 4 5	Offers untimed tests if indicated
1 2 3 4 5	Reduces number of problems
1 2 3 4 5	Provides direct instruction for the use of calculators

Science	
1 2 3 4 5	Includes hands-on, interactive experiences
1 2 3 4 5	Offers activities that incorporate problem solving and real-life investigations with a purpose and an end product
1 2 3 4 5	Uses a thematic approach that allows for students to direct their search for knowledge and answers
1 2 3 4 5	Incorporates simulations
1 2 3 4 5	Integrates visual and performing arts
1 2 3 4 5	Focuses on science process objectives
1 2 3 4 5	Gives students graphic organizers to support note taking

	Social Studies
1 2 3 4 5	Holds students accountable for learning the historical, economic, political, geographic, and cultural content standards
1 2 3 4 5	Constructs understandings through systems of processing information, critical thinking, and problem solving
1 2 3 4 5	Uses thematic units
1 2 3 4 5	Incorporates simulations
1 2 3 4 5	Includes hands-on activities and projects
1 2 3 4 5	Uses various forms of media
1 2 3 4 5	Integrates visual and performing arts
1 2 3 4 5	Provides extension/enrichment activities

	Assessment
1 2 3 4 5	Supports student/teacher collaboration on the evaluation/assessment methods and tools
1 2 3 4 5	Bases evaluations on instruction and reflects the key concepts and basic understandings that are the focus of the curriculum
1 2 3 4 5	Provides objectives, study guides, vocabulary, memory strategies, acceptable responses, support, and clarification for embedded questions
1 2 3 4 5	Uses differentiation
1 2 3 4 5	Allows for audiotape responses
1 2 3 4 5	Allows students to use graphic organizers in lieu of paragraph responses
1 2 3 4 5	Offers students alternative products like creating a model or giving a speech

Note. Adapted from unpublished charts by Larry March and Martha Abolins. Reprinted with permission.

Tools 55–58: Aligning Instruction With Strengths

Tool 58: Instructional Strategies That Work!

Directions: Use this chart as a reference for strength-based lesson planning. It is crucial to select strategies that will help the student(s) master the objective for the lesson.

2-4-6-8	Given a topic or question, students pair up to brainstorm, then form groups of four to share/add ideas, then form groups of six to share/add ideas, then form groups of eight to share/add ideas.
3 Before Me	A management strategy where students are taught to check three resources before seeking out the teacher for assistance. For example, ask a peer, reread the directions, and check the word wall.
10-2	After every 10 minutes of instruction (approximately), provide students with a 2-minute reflection/processing/ debriefing time to clarify concepts.
A-B-C Summary	Based on a topic or unit of study, students are asked to identify a key term for each letter of the alphabet.
Acrostic Summary	Based on a topic or unit of study, students are asked to identify a key term for each letter of a word.
Advanced Organizers	A concept map or other organizer that visually displays the content of a unit of study.
Affinity Diagram	Students brainstorm ideas in a given topic, then sort them into categories.
Anchor Activities	Ongoing, engaging assignments (linked to the curriculum and their interests) that students can work on fairly independently.
Around the World Summary	Standing in a circle, passing a globe (or other icon), each student takes a turn sharing an important idea, connection, or insight related to the lesson.
Bookmark for Guided Reading	Students are given a bookmark with focus questions or a graphic organizer to complete while reading.
Buzz Group	Students are placed into small groups to discuss a topic or question prior to whole-group discussion.
Capture Sheet	A note-taking device or graphic organizer that corresponds to the lesson and requires minimal writing.

Card Sort	Students sort words, ideas, pictures, and so on into predetermined categories, then analyze and justify their groupings and compare them to other ways of thinking.
Carousel Brainstorm	Posters with different prompts or questions are posted around the room and small groups of students travel from one to the next, recording ideas or discussing until they have visited all of them, continuously adding to the previous groups' ideas.
Choice Board	Students make a selection from a row of selections (based on readiness, interest, or learning style). Sometimes a tic-tac-toe format is used.
Coffee Talk	Students are given a scenario where they are to "mingle" in the classroom, discussing a topic or idea. Cue cards are recommended.
Compacting	A system designed to adapt the regular curriculum to meet the needs of above-average students by either eliminating work that has been mastered previously or streamlining work that may be mastered more quickly.
Concept Map	A visual representation of a concept and the relationships within the concept as it relates to other disciplines and topics. Shows the big picture of a unit and how it fits with previous units.
Contracts	Written agreements between teachers and students that outline what students will learn, how they will learn it, in what period of time, and how they will be evaluated. Contracts allow for students to plan their own learning and take responsibility.
Cubing	A cube with six commands (may be tiered so that some students have different cubes) and prompts that describe a task related to the topic/unit.
Discussion Starter Sticks/ Cards	Each student selects or is given a discussion prompt on sticks or cards and then discusses.
Doctor Is In	A management strategy where students sign up for teacher support but return to their work while they are waiting.
Expert Groups	Students are grouped together to learn about and report on a topic or question.
Fishbowl Discussion	Students sit in two circles, an inner and outer circle. The inner circle discusses a topic/question while the outer circle observes, takes notes, and reflects.

Tools 55–58: Aligning Instruction With Strengths

Flexible Grouping	The use of ongoing assessment to inform temporary instructional grouping that changes frequently based on student readiness, interests, and learning styles.
Flow Chart	A graphic representation of actions or steps in a process that gives students a visual model to follow.
Four Corners	Four ideas, quotes, or possible responses are placed in the four corners of the room and students move to the area that corresponds to their beliefs, opinion, or response. Discussion ensues.
Graphic Organizers	A visual and graphic display that depicts the relationships between facts, terms, and/or ideas within a learning task.
Illustrated Note Taking	Students take picture notes or doodles as opposed to traditional notes. The teacher provides key words or an outline and space for the student to draw.
The Important Thing	Students identify the most important attribute of a concept along with several other critical attributes.
In a Nutshell	Students identify the most salient information in a given concept.
Independent Study	Students work independently to research an issue, solve a problem, or complete a project to enrich a unit of study.
Interest Centers	Students work at teacher-developed centers using task cards to explore a topic in depth.
Interest Surveys	Students answer questions to identify interests (in general or related to a unit of study).
Jigsaw	Students start in groups and each person takes a different job or focus. They regroup into job-alike groups to perform their task and then regroup into their original groups where they serve as experts and share their learning with the group.
K-W-L	Students identify what they know, what they want to know, and what they learned about a topic or concept. Can extend by adding columns to the chart (e.g., What I Still Want to Know or K-W-L-S).
Learning Centers	A classroom area that contains a collection of activities or materials designed to teach, reinforce, or extend a skill or concept.
Learning Menus	Students are given choices of tasks for their main course (required), side dishes (select a few), and desserts (optional extensions).

Learning Style Surveys	Students respond to questions that help them to determine their learning style strengths and preferences that can inform tasks/grouping (e.g., My Way Inventory).
Marking Text	Students are given symbols that define ways for the reader to engage with the text (! = surprising, ? = raises a question, ☺ = I like this).
Metaphorical Associations	Students identify a list of things that are like the topic or concept and explain their thinking. For example, teaching is like popping corn because some corn takes longer than others to pop.
MI Summarizer	Students choose from a variety of tasks based on their preferred MI.
Most Difficult First	Students are given the opportunity to demonstrate mastery on the most difficult items first to free up time for alternative activities.
OCI Chart	Given a problem or issue, students identify the Opportunities, Challenges, and Ideas for solving the problem.
One Word Summary	Students identify one word that represents a topic or concept.
Paired Verbal Fluency	Students pair up and each student is given a specific amount of time to talk uninterrupted about the concept while the other listens. Several rounds are done.
Paul's Reasoning Wheel	A model for students to organize their approach to thinking about a problem or issue.
Picture Vocabulary	Students generate (or the teacher provides as a scaffold) vocabulary cards with an image that captures the essence of the word's meaning.
Placemat	Words, pictures, quotes, and graphics are splashed around a legal-size piece of paper and students are asked to connect them and make meaning where they can.
PNI Chart	Students are asked to determine the Positive, Negative, and Interesting aspects of a topic, issue, or concept.
Puzzle Pieces	A piece of paper for each key term, picture, and example is cut into pieces and students assemble the puzzles to create meaning.
Question Cubes	Question starters on cubes are rolled and students generate questions (ranging from simple to complex) on a topic.

Tools 55–58: Aligning Instruction With Strengths

RAFT	Students select from various Roles, Audiences, Formats, and Topics to create a prompt of their choosing.
SCAMPER	A creative thinking strategy that gets students to transform ideas: Substitute, Combine, Adapt, Minimize/Magnify, Put to other uses, Eliminate, Reverse, Rearrange.
See-Hear-Feel Chart	Students record observations based on these three senses. It can be used to teach abstract concepts (e.g., oppression) by helping students make concrete observations about the idea.
Shared Inquiry	Students participate in teacher-facilitated discussions regarding a short story, responding to interpretive questions to build understanding of text.
Six Hats Thinking	Six colored hats represent six ways of thinking about a problem or issue. This approach teaches students to be metacognitive and to be strategic about critical thinking and problem solving.
Stoplight Strategy	Students use color-coded flags (or cups or sticky notes on the desk) to indicate that they are good-to-go (green), need clarification (yellow), or need help (red).
Swap Meet	Students record three ideas on three index cards and circulate around the room, "swapping" ideas until they have exchanged all of their ideas for new ones.
Synectics	Students are asked to compare two things (one of which is usually the curricular concept or topic and one of which is an object that it would not ordinarily be compared to) in order to reexamine the concept.
Think Alouds	The teacher models a task, talking aloud to himself so that the students can see how the teacher thinks through the task.
Think-Pair-Share	Students think individually, then talk with a partner, then share ideas out loud with the class.
Tiering	An instructional approach designed to have students of different readiness levels, interests, or learning styles work with appropriately differentiated tasks/content.
Top 10 List	Students determine/rank the most important ideas out of a bank of ideas based on established criteria for importance.
Visualization/ Mental Imagery	Students are directed to visualize a story, concept, or idea to develop their understanding and to support memory.

Whip-Around	The teacher whips around the room, collecting a quick idea from each person.
Word Banks	Specific to the task, word banks scaffold students' thinking and spelling.
Word Splash	Words related to a concept are splashed on a poster or chart and students are asked to predict what they will be learning about.

Tools 55–58: Aligning Instruction With Strengths

Tools 59–64: Writing

Writing is one of the most complex tasks a student is asked to do, yet it is a beautiful mode of self-expression to which many of these students are drawn. They love to be creative and they want to express their ideas. The tools in this section are designed to help you understand the needs of these students as they relate to writing and to teach them to better communicate their vast knowledge and limitless creativity through writing.

Tips

✓ *Tool 59: Student Tool: Solving the Mystery: Why Is Writing So Hard?* This rating scale helps students to "decode" their writing weaknesses.

✓ *Tool 60: Tips for Teaching Writing.* This list provides insights for critical elements needed to teach bright kids how to be better writers.

✓ *Tool 61: Supporting Struggling Writers.* These ideas will help you consider ways to support students with writing prior to the lesson or task.

✓ *Tool 62: Exciting Writing Prompts.* Do you have a student who hates writing? Entice him or her with one of these writing prompts that require creativity, originality, or a unique perspective.

✓ *Tool 63: Written Work Feedback.* These students need specific praise and feedback on their writing in order to understand what they are doing well and what they need to do to improve. Use this tool to supplement your quantitative rubrics and to conference with the student following each assignment. Separating out content and mechanics feedback is important because these students often have great content and weak mechanics.

✓ *Tool 64: Writing Skills Rubric.* Rubrics are effective tools to use with students to evaluate written work. This rubric may be used as is or adapted.

Tool 59: Student Tool
Solving the Mystery: Why Is Writing So Hard?

Hand and Finger Control	Always	Mostly	Sometimes	Not at All
My hand gets very tired when I write.				
I have an unusual way of holding a pencil or pen.				
I write too slowly.				
My print is better than my cursive.				
My cursive is better than my print.				
Forming letters is more difficult for me than for other kids.				
Putting Ideas Into Words	**Always**	**Mostly**	**Sometimes**	**Not at All**
I find it hard to get my ideas into words when I speak.				
I make many grammar mistakes when I write.				
It takes me a long time to get my ideas on paper.				
I have trouble spelling so I only use easy words.				
Coming Up With Ideas	**Always**	**Mostly**	**Sometimes**	**Not at All**
I find it hard to decide what I want to write about.				
It is difficult to know what to write or include in a report.				
It is hard to come up with my own ideas or stories.				
It's hard to write about my opinions.				

Tools 59–64: Writing

Tools 59–64: Writing

Remembering	Always	Mostly	Sometimes	Not at All
It's hard for me to remember my ideas while I am writing.				
My ideas are much better when I speak than when I write.				
Spelling makes it hard for me to write.				
Organizing	Always	Mostly	Sometimes	Not at All
It's hard for me to get started on writing.				
I get confused when I am writing.				
I have trouble getting my thoughts down in the right order.				
I don't think or plan much about what I'm going to write; I just start writing.				
I often don't have the materials I need to start writing (like paper, pencil, books).				
Concentrating	Always	Mostly	Sometimes	Not at All
It can be really hard to get started with a writing assignment.				
I have trouble handling all of the little details in writing.				
I feel bored and tired when I have to do a lot of writing.				
I race through a writing assignment without much thinking or planning.				
I skip proofreading. When I'm done, I'm done.				

Note. Adapted from Levine, 2004.

Circle any of these things that might/do help you to write better.

- Using the computer

- Using graphic organizers

- Talking out my ideas before I start

- Checking in with an adult periodically

- Using spell checker

- Having step-by-step written directions

- Seeing an example

- Having word banks

- Having extra time

Tools 59–64: Writing

Tool 60: Tips for Teaching Writing

✓ Students with learning difficulties often hate to write but love to speak their mind, so writing assignments that allow them to evaluate, give an opinion, or persuade someone often get them excited.

✓ They often love creative writing assignments that allow them to play with words and ideas, are more open-ended, and allow them to develop a unique voice.

✓ Set high expectations for content, and if you must grade for mechanics, give each paper at least two grades (one for content and one for mechanics).

✓ These students love to write for authentic audiences such as the school newspaper and love to share their favorite pieces with people other than you.

✓ To entice these students to write, provide them with tons of choice. They want to be able to choose what to write about and how to communicate their ideas.

✓ Don't forget technology. Many students think they hate to write, but what they really hate is handwriting or rewriting all of those drafts!

✓ Praise, praise, and praise again. If a student is a reluctant writer, she probably feels terrible about her writing and only notices the problems. Emphasize the positive.

✓ Give specific feedback. Once you have praised the good in the writing, give the student two or three ways to improve the writing. Be concrete by saying things such as, "Add three adjectives," "Expand this sentence," or "Add one more reason."

✓ Teach the writing process. This allows the student to see how to break down the writing and helps him to not be so overwhelmed by the enormity of the task.

✓ Teach the 6+1 Traits of Writing explicitly. By focusing on one or two traits at a time, you help the student focus on improving specific skills and not get so overwhelmed.

Tool 61: Supporting Struggling Writers

Directions: Prior to a unit or lesson, identify accommodations related to writing such as the following:

✓ *Graphic Organizer/Outline First:* The organizer/outline must fit the task and the student often needs instruction in how to complete the graphic organizer and how to convert that into a piece of writing.

✓ *Verbal Prewriting Conference:* After everyone has received directions or before introducing the assignment, sit down with the student for a minute and ask him to tell you his ideas. Many kids need to see (or speak) the whole thing before they can start.

✓ *Quiet Area to Work:* Give the student a study carrel or headphones (with or without music), or allow her to work in the media center, resource room, or computer lab.

✓ *Task Analysis/Checklists:* If the student has difficulty breaking down a large assignment into its component parts, or seems overwhelmed by the enormity of the task, make (with the student) a simple checklist. Set deadlines/timelines for each step.

✓ *Frequent Checks/Hurdle Help:* Despite prewriting activities and support, most twice-exceptional students will require some checking in with the teacher.

✓ *Anchor Papers:* Seeing model papers (both good and bad) helps the student visualize the end product and understand exactly what you want.

✓ *Computer/Software:* Word processing software, Inspiration, Co:Writer, Write:OutLoud, and/or Draft:Builder would all be appropriate technology tools (depending on the student).

✓ *Alternatives:* If writing is not the purpose of an assignment, find another way for your struggling writers to demonstrate their knowledge through their strengths.

Tools 59–64: Writing

Tool 62: Exciting Writing Prompts

✓ Take a "boring" poem or piece of short text, tear it apart, and make it better!

✓ Start a novel (or story) of your own. Use a story starter as needed. Create an outline or storyboard and then begin!

✓ Reread a favorite picture book or story and then rewrite it with a twist! Write from the perspective of a different character, give the story a new setting (time and place), or change the plot in some interesting way.

✓ Imagine you have found a time machine that will allow you to go back in time for 1 hour. Where and when would you go? Why? What would you see, hear, feel, and experience? What would be one thing you would bring back with you and why? How could your actions on this trip impact the future?

✓ Write a new ending to the mystery (story, fairy tale).

✓ Outline (then write if you'd like) a sequel to a story or book you really enjoyed.

✓ What is the best place to go to relax (play, shop, eat)? Justify your response.

✓ Create an invention that solves a problem that you or others have. Describe the invention and explain how this invention would improve or change people's lives. Write a letter to a company owner convincing him to invest in your invention.

✓ Write a story titled "The Great Escape" from the point of view of a turkey on Thanksgiving Day.

✓ Imagine that you are an alien from another planet and you are on an information-gathering mission to Earth. You have never seen many of the objects used here on Earth. Select a common, everyday object and write a description using your five senses (what does it look like, smell like, sound like, taste like, feel like) and explain how the humans use this object and for what purpose. Your classmates will attempt to identify this object based on your writing.

✓ Write about your weekend (break, holiday, vacation) that includes five facts and one fib. We'll see if we can sniff out the lie!

✓ Your principal has decided that field trips (recess, art) are a waste of time. Survey your classmates to determine the academic value of field trips and write the principal a letter persuading him or her not to cut field trips from the calendar.

✓ What if . . . birds didn't fly? Elephants lived in cities? People didn't have fingers? Columbus was never born? Brainstorm as many ways as you can think of that this would change things and then write about it.

✓ Describe the color _____ without using any color words, but using your five senses and figurative language (similes, metaphors, personification). We'll try to guess your color.

✓ Describe an emotion (love, anger, sadness, fear, happiness). What causes it? How does it feel? What are some symbols of that emotion? If it were tangible, what would it look like, feel like, taste like, smell like? What are the pros and cons of feeling that way? Be as descriptive as possible so that someone who has never experienced this emotion can begin to understand how it might feel.

✓ Write an obituary/epitaph/funeral speech for a character that tells the important events from his or her life and gives a sense of the personality traits of the character.

✓ Explain _____ from the point of view of _____ (brushing your teeth/a toothbrush, snow days/a snowman, walking the dog/a dog).

✓ Brainstorm a list of words that come to mind when you think of _____. Work with a partner or group to identify more words. Now, write a poem or a paragraph about the topic without using *any* of those words.

✓ *Extreme Makeover: Home Edition* has selected your family for a home renovation! Sketch your ideal bedroom. Then, write a clear description of the room so that the team will be able to create your new room just the way you want it!

✓ Create a comic strip or graphic novel that tells a funny, scary, or adventurous story.

Tools 59–64: Writing

Tool 63: Written Work Feedback

Student Name: _____

Assignment: _____

Content Considerations:
- ✓ Does the piece contain enough information? Does it make sense? Does it respond to all parts of the prompt/question?
- ✓ Are there adequate details and supporting information?
- ✓ If informational writing, are the facts accurate? If persuasive writing, are the arguments supported and explained? If narrative writing, is there a beginning, a middle, and an end?
- ✓ Does the writing engage and interest the reader?
- ✓ Are sentences varied? Is word choice explicit and varied?

Strengths	Things to Work On

Mechanics Considerations:
- ✓ Is the piece capitalized and punctuated properly?
- ✓ Is the grammar accurate?
- ✓ Does the paper have a heading (name and date) and title?
- ✓ Is the first line of each paragraph indented?
- ✓ Is the paper clearly organized so that the reader can understand the content?

Strengths	Things to Work On

Tool 64: Writing Skills Rubric

Ideas and Development   1   2   3   4
- ❏ The written work reflects clear thinking and planning.
- ❏ The written work is an appropriate response to the prompt.

Organization   1   2   3   4
- ❏ The organization is appropriate for the response to the prompt.
- ❏ There is a clear introduction, body, and conclusion.
- ❏ There are transitions between paragraphs.

Voice   1   2   3   4
- ❏ The writer's voice is individual and engaging.
- ❏ The reader senses the person behind the words.
- ❏ The writer's words cause a reaction in the reader.

Word Choice   1   2   3   4
- ❏ The writer's word selection and usage are clear.
- ❏ The writer uses vivid language and active verbs to enhance meaning.

Sentence Fluency   1   2   3   4
- ❏ Sentences vary in both structure and length and include both compound and complex sentences.
- ❏ Dependent clauses help vary the sentence structure.

Conventions   1   2   3   4
- ❏ Spelling is correct.
- ❏ Punctuation is correct.
- ❏ Capitalization is correct.

Total: _____

Grade: _____

Tools 65–67: Organization

Organization is a huge obstacle for these students. Many lack the executive functioning skills necessary for planning and executing tasks such as classwork, daily homework, and long-term projects. Others struggle with the organization of materials and time. The tools in this section are designed to help you support and improve these areas of difficulty.

Tips

- ✓ *Tool 65: Tips for Teaching Organization.* Refer to these ideas for ways to help your students improve their organizational skills.
- ✓ *Tool 66: Student Tool: Task Analysis for Assignments.* Students can benefit greatly from doing a task analysis. Teachers should conference with the students or a small group of students after a multistep assignment is given.
- ✓ *Tool 67: Parent Partnership Piece: Strategies to Avoid Homework Headaches!* Share these ideas with parents to improve their ability to support their child with homework.

Tool 65: Tips for Teaching Organization

✓ Connect schoolwork to passions, strengths, and interests whenever possible so that the students *care* to stay on top of their workload.

✓ Repeat directions and have the students put the directions in their own words to ensure they completely understand. If you just ask if they understand, these students will say "Yes."

✓ Keep the workload reasonable; reduce the workload so that students can accomplish the expected tasks in the same timeframe that other students would be expected to work.

✓ Supply structure and predictability of routines. Post routines and schedules and provide notice of transitions and changes.

✓ Provide a verbal or nonverbal cue for "active listening" (use an active listening chart to explicitly teach this behavioral expectation).

✓ Break down multistep and long-term tasks and set mini-deadlines. Check the students' progress frequently. Model and teach this process until students can do it by themselves.

✓ Make frequent progress checks during independent work. Provide verbal and visual prompts and cues to task.

✓ Teach students to look around and to notice what others are doing. They can use this strategy to cue themselves to work.

✓ Provide a second set of books and core course materials for home use so that forgetting these materials doesn't disrupt the learning process.

✓ Teach students how to conduct an assignment task analysis and self-evaluate progress through a task (see Tool 66).

✓ Provide visual models (photographs, drawings, charts, labels) and time each day to organize binders, cubbies, desks, and/or lockers.

✓ Provide time periodically (weekly, monthly, quarterly) for students to clean out their binders and give them a safe place to file "old papers" where they can get them if they need them.

✓ Support the use of a planner, monitored by teachers for completion and accuracy/legibility of information.

✓ Have students estimate the amount of time needed to complete a task, then use a stopwatch or timer to figure the actual time used. This will often help students more realistically estimate the time needed in the future on similar tasks.

✓ Use checklists for organizing binders, prioritizing and completing tasks, turning in work, and morning and pack-up routines.

✓ Teach students a variety of ways to manage their class materials and let them choose what works for them.

Tool 66: Student Tool
Task Analysis for Assignments

Effective planning is very important! A task analysis is a way to think about any job. The following is a step-by-step plan that may help you as you break a big assignment into small steps.

_____ Step 1: Decide on exactly what you must do.
- ❏ Find the key words in the directions.
- ❏ Look carefully at the exact words used.
- ❏ Say aloud (to yourself) what you must do.
- ❏ Read the directions one more time.

_____ Step 2: Decide on the number of steps needed to complete the task.
- ❏ Make a list of all of the steps needed to accomplish the task.
- ❏ Rank the steps in the order of their importance.

_____ Step 3: Decide on the amount of time each step will take you to do.
- ❏ Write your steps in the order you ranked them.
- ❏ Record the amount of time each task will take you to do.

_____ Step 4: Create a schedule.
- ❏ Count the number of days you have to do the task.
- ❏ Look at a calendar.
- ❏ Write the day you begin and the deadline date on the calendar.
- ❏ Plan a time for every step of the task. Some tasks take less time; some tasks may take more time.
- ❏ Make changes in your time plan when necessary.

_____ Step 5: Start!
- ❏ Stay on your schedule.
- ❏ Record the day you finish each task.
- ❏ Make changes to your schedule or plan if needed.
- ❏ Get help immediately if there is a problem you cannot solve.

_____ Step 6: Finish the task.
- ❏ Complete it on time—meet the deadline.
- ❏ Evaluate your finished assignment.
- ❏ Reward yourself for a job well done.

Tools 65–67: Organization

Tool 67: Parent Partnership Piece
Strategies to Avoid Homework Headaches!

Dear Parent,

Sometimes homework can be a challenge! On top of reading and writing help, your child may need assistance getting started, figuring out what to do first and next, paying attention to directions, checking his or her work, and getting his or her work back to school and turned in. Below are some ideas that might reduce the stress surrounding homework in your home.

Getting Ready

With your child:

❏ Establish a set time for homework. Make sure down time is included in the afterschool schedule.

❏ Set up a homework area that is quiet, comfortable, and has easy access to resources (e.g., computer, dictionary, calculator, textbooks, pens and pencils, paper).

❏ Review the daily and long-term assignments your child must work on that day. Make a list and prioritize the order in which items will be completed. Some kids need to tackle the harder assignments first when they are fresh, while others need to "warm up" with an easy assignment. Prioritize based on your child's learning style.

❏ Set goals for completion of each task and use a timer to see if your child can beat his or her best time.

Getting Started

❏ Have your child write his or her name and a title on all papers.

❏ Read the directions with your child before beginning an assignment. Verbally check for understanding and clarify the directions and expectations as needed.

❏ Encourage your child to work independently. Periodically check on his or her progress. Tell your child how to signal you if he or she needs help.

Finishing Up

❏ Teach your child to complete the assignment and then check over his or her work when it is complete.

❏ When you or your child notice that he or she has made a mistake, encourage your child to try again or to make a note to ask the teacher for help the next day.

❏ Encourage your child to review the directions to make sure he or she has done what was asked.

❏ Support or monitor your child as he or she puts the papers where they belong. Having a special homework folder or place is a good idea.

❏ Celebrate successes (e.g., increased independence, asking for help) in order to give your child feedback on his or her homework habits.

We all know homework can be challenging for parents and children. Please let me know what you find works best for your child and when particular kinds of assignments are causing "homework headaches."

Sincerely,

Tools 65–67: Organization

Tools 68–70:
Reading

Bright but struggling readers are often below grade level in some areas (typically decoding and fluency), on grade level in some areas (independent reading comprehension), and above grade level in other areas (vocabulary, use of context and background knowledge, listening comprehension). These students require a balanced approach to reading that addresses their strengths and acknowledges their need to access higher-level stories and text while also intervening in their areas of weakness. The tools in this section are designed to help you provide reading instruction that hits all of these points.

Tips

- ✓ *Tool 68: Tips for Teaching Reading.* These are important components to consider when designing reading instruction and interventions for bright but struggling readers.
- ✓ *Tool 69: Supporting Struggling Readers.* This checklist can be used to determine necessary reading accommodations for a student (in general or for a given task).
- ✓ *Tool 70: Student Tool: Skills for Using a Textbook.* Use this guide to help kids use textbooks in and out of class.

Tool 68: Tips for Teaching Reading

Acknowledging Strengths
- ✓ Ensure the majority of the reading day is focused on high-level literature and nonfiction.
- ✓ Create a classroom library that includes a variety of text levels and genres. These students often love fantasy, science fiction, and adventure books. Consider student interests.
- ✓ Set up a comfortable listening/reading area (e.g., bean bag chairs, couches, carpets) with audio/recorded books and players (e.g., MP3 players, computer, tape recorders, CD players). Don't forget the headsets!

Turning Weaknesses Into Strengths
- ✓ Acknowledge that remedial instruction focuses on a student's weaknesses and that it will be hard and at times frustrating. It may at times seem "babyish" to students, but it will help them to make real progress in this area.
- ✓ Measure the student's baseline reading performance using preassessments or placement tests (or an informal reading inventory) and show him the results. Candidly share information about his current reading level and where you expect him to be by the end of your time together. Document progress and share it with the student. Have him chart his progress.
- ✓ Set goals together in terms of rate of progress.
- ✓ Develop games that make the learning fun to supplement the reading program.
- ✓ Let the student be the teacher when he has mastered a skill.
- ✓ Incorporate movement and hands-on activities (e.g., card sorts, matching).
- ✓ Set up a "beat your best" competitive element that lets the group (or individual students) earn incentives based on its progress.
- ✓ Ensure that the pace is tailored to the students' learning. Move on when they are ready.
- ✓ Let them discover the rules of reading (e.g., by showing examples and nonexamples of closed syllables).
- ✓ Generalize the skills they are learning to "real" reading and writing by pointing out words they should be able to read or spell. Cue them to use learned strategies during this "real" reading and writing.
- ✓ Ensure that they don't overrely on decoding efforts by reinforcing their use of context clues, background knowledge, and vocabulary when reading text.

Tools 68–70: Reading

Tool 69: Supporting Struggling Readers

Directions: Prior to a unit or lesson, identify accommodations that will help your students to access challenging text.

✓ *Highlight Critical Information:* Prior to copying the text, underline or highlight key terms and ideas. This can be done for some or all students.

✓ *Preview Vocabulary:* Identify key terms that students may have difficulty decoding (e.g., multisyllabic, new/unknown, nonphonetic) and highlight these words in the text. Before reading, point out these words, read them to students, and discuss the meaning. This will increase the chances that your students will be able to make meaning from the text.

✓ *Text Preview:* Give a brief, oral preview of the main ideas in the text. This will help the students to form a "big picture" about the meaning of the text.

✓ *Adequate Time or Provide in Advance:* Provide time for all students to finish reading. If a student constantly needs excessive extra time to finish reading, try the read aloud strategy below.

✓ *Read Aloud:* Try partner reading, where you pair a stronger reader with a weaker reader and have them take turns or have the stronger reader read and have the other student highlight key ideas in the text. Even with older students, it is often appropriate for the teacher (or a designated student) to read aloud to a group of students. A struggling reader should never be *required* to read aloud for the class.

✓ *Assistive Technology:* Many technology options exist to support struggling readers. See Tool 77 for ideas. In addition, audiobooks and recorded text can be obtained to help struggling readers. For audiobooks, check local libraries and sites like Amazon.com and Audible.com. For recorded text, visit http://www.rfbd.org and http://www.bookshare.com.

Tool 70: Student Tool
Skills for Using a Textbook

Here are some quick tips for studying from a textbook:

Have a purpose for reading!

- ❑ What do you need to learn?
- ❑ Why do you need to learn it?
- ❑ Where will you find the information you need?

Use good strategies!

- ❑ List the things you want to know.
- ❑ Check out the Table of Contents.
- ❑ Check out the topic headings in boldface print.
- ❑ Take notes.
- ❑ Review your notes.

Survey the chapter!

- ❑ Read the first two paragraphs.
- ❑ Read the subtopics (usually in boldface print).
- ❑ Read the last two paragraphs.
- ❑ Look at the graphics (pictures, diagrams, maps).
- ❑ Read the captions for the graphics.
- ❑ Now go back to the beginning and read the chapter.

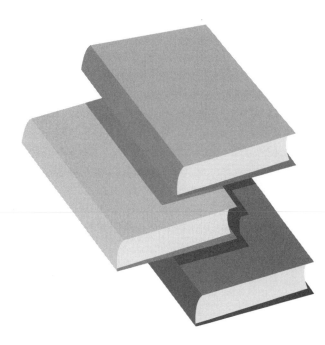

Tools 68–70: Reading

Tools 71–78: Planning Tools

Teaching is a science, but it is also an art. Your expertise as an educator will guide you as you analyze, evaluate, and synthesize all of the concepts in this book. This section is dedicated to providing you with tools that will support your instructional planning as you strive to incorporate best practices.

Tips

✓ *Tool 71: Planning Higher Level Questions and Tasks.* Use this tool to help you develop questions and tasks based on Bloom's taxonomy for your units and lessons.

✓ *Tool 72: Lesson Planning With the W.O.R.M. in Mind.* When you plan with common obstacles in mind (**W**riting, **O**rganization, **R**eading, and **M**emory) you are able to develop lessons that circumvent weaknesses and allow for student success.

✓ *Tool 73: Unit Planning With MI in Mind.* Proactively considering multiple intelligences will ensure that all of your students will be able to work through their areas of strength to master content and demonstrate their knowledge.

✓ *Tool 74: Differentiated Lesson Planning Template.* This tool will help you to develop lessons that address students' varied learning styles, readiness, and interests.

✓ *Tool 75: Differentiation Pyramid.* This graphic conceptualizes how differentiation might look in your classroom. Use the template to support development of differentiated tasks.

✓ *Tool 76: Student Tool: Instead of . . . Can I . . . ?* Why must we always write? There are lots of ways for students to show what they know. Use this tool to allow your students to advocate for strength-based alternatives to traditional (paper and pencil) assignments.

✓ *Tool 77: Assistive Technology Options.* Technology offers many ways to support students with learning differences. Use this tool to help you select appropriate software for your student. If you are unfamiliar with the products described, consult with your school's special educator, technology/computer support person, and/or occupational therapist.

✓ *Tool 78: Unit Planning Template.* There are so many components to consider when designing instruction for these students. This template will keep you focused on the "big picture" and ensure that you consider each factor as you plan your units.

Tool 71: Planning Higher Level Questions and Tasks

1. What is the content for your questioning (topic or unit of study)?
2. What is your goal or purpose for asking these questions (objective)?

Remembering
Identifying, remembering, recalling, and/or restating information.

Possible Question Starters
- What is the definition for . . .?
- What happened after . . .?
- What were the facts involved . . .?
- What are the characteristics of . . .?
- Which is true or false . . .?
- How many . . .?
- What are the key ideas or events . . .?
- Who, what, when, where . . .?

Key Words

❏	define	❏	memorize
❏	find	❏	recall
❏	label	❏	recite
❏	list	❏	remember
❏	match	❏	select

Write a remembering question or prompt:

Understanding
Demonstrating understanding of ideas and concepts.

Possible Question Starters

- Why are these ideas similar . . .?
- What are the key events in the story . . .?
- What do you think could happen . . .?
- How are these ideas different . . .?
- What caused . . .?
- What does _____ symbolize . . .?
- What is the meaning of . . .?
- What is the main idea of . . .?
- Why is this important . . .?

Key Words

❏ clarify	❏ identify
❏ conclude	❏ illustrate
❏ connect	❏ infer
❏ describe	❏ interpret
❏ discuss	❏ paraphrase
❏ estimate	❏ restate
❏ explain	❏ sequence
❏ give examples	❏ translate

Write an understanding question or prompt:

Applying
Using information studied and mastered in new situations and in new ways.

Possible Question Starters
- Where else have you seen this . . .?
- Which factors would you change . . .?
- How could you demonstrate this concept . . .?
- Could this have happened in . . .?
- What questions would you ask . . .?
- How would you organize . . .?
- Which one is most like . . .?

Key Words

❑	apply	❑	modify
❑	build	❑	organize
❑	classify	❑	predict
❑	demonstrate	❑	prove
❑	dramatize	❑	revise
❑	extend	❑	simulate
❑	illustrate	❑	solve
❑	interpret	❑	use

Write an applying question or prompt:

Analyzing

Identifying components and distinguishing between parts of information, ideas, or products.

Possible Question Starters

- What are the parts of . . . ?
- What steps are involved in . . . ?
- What other conclusions can you draw . . . ?
- What are the similarities and differences . . . ?
- What are some possible solutions . . . ?
- What is the relationship between . . . ?
- What was the problem with . . . ?
- Why does this work . . . ?
- Why did the character . . . ?

Key Words

- ❏ arrange
- ❏ categorize
- ❏ compare
- ❏ contrast
- ❏ deduce
- ❏ determine
- ❏ diagram
- ❏ distinguish
- ❏ experiment
- ❏ find
- ❏ inquire
- ❏ isolate
- ❏ observe
- ❏ organize
- ❏ proofread
- ❏ survey
- ❏ take apart

Write an analyzing question or prompt:

Evaluating
Making reasoned judgments and decisions about an idea, issue, or topic.

Possible Question Starters

- What is your opinion about . . . and why?
- What should happen . . .?
- What is the best solution for . . . and why?
- What are the chances . . .?
- What is the bigger bargain . . . and why?
- Which is the best . . . the worst . . . and why?
- How would you rank or prioritize these items . . . and why?
- What evidence supports . . .?
- What is right/wrong with . . .?
- Why does the solution . . .?

Key Words:

❏ appraise	❏ justify
❏ assess	❏ persuade
❏ conclude	❏ prioritize
❏ critique	❏ rank
❏ determine	❏ rate
❏ disprove/prove	❏ recommend
❏ grade	❏ select
❏ judge	❏ verify

Write an evaluating question or prompt:

Creating
Creating new solutions, ideas, or products.

Possible Question Starters

- What is another way ...?
- How could you design ...?
- How might you use ...?
- What might happen if ...?
- Who might ...?
- When might ...?
- What ideas can you add ...?
- What is another example of ...?
- Why is there a reason to ...?

Key Words

❑	add to	❑	formulate
❑	alter	❑	hypothesize
❑	arrange	❑	illustrate
❑	brainstorm	❑	imagine
❑	combine	❑	invent
❑	compose	❑	modify
❑	connect	❑	predict
❑	construct	❑	rename
❑	delete	❑	resolve
❑	design	❑	suggest
❑	elaborate	❑	visualize
❑	extend	❑	write

Write a creating question or prompt:

Tool 72: Lesson Planning With the W.O.R.M. in Mind

Directions: Complete the student characteristics column for each student with learning difficulties. Make photocopies and then use the template and Tool 40 to adapt your lessons and to identify necessary accommodations for this student.

Student Characteristics	Obstacles to Success	Accommodations/Adaptations Needed for Success
Writing Strengths: **Writing Weaknesses:**		❏ Accommodate the student (circle): o copies of notes o graphic organizers o extra time o grade for content only o verbal elaboration o frames/outlines o verbal prewriting conference o quiet area to work o frequent checks and "hurdle help" o task analysis o checklists o rubrics o examples of model papers o adequate space to write or attach paper o words and phrases instead of sentences o visual clutter reduced o fewer problems/questions assigned o alternative assignments o writing partner or buddy o computer time o electronic spellers ❏ Adapt the lesson:

Tools 71–78: Planning Tools

Student Characteristics	Obstacles to Success	Accommodations/Adaptations Needed for Success

Organizational Strengths:
 	
Organizational Weaknesses:
		❏ Accommodate the student (circle):
		  o plan book is initialed
		  o calendar
		  o homework website
		  o homework buddy
		  o frequent progress reports
		  o daily verbal check-in
		  o task analysis and mini-deadlines
		  o papers labeled (HW, CW, notes) and place assigned for each
		  o prompt to submit work
		  o reduced workload
		  o ongoing list of assignments and due dates
		  o color coding
		  o accordion files
		  o time and cues to file things
		  o time to clean out
		  o storage bin for "old stuff"
		  o supplies kept in classroom
		  o copies of texts for home/class
		  o study guides/outlines
		❏ Adapt the lesson:

Reading Strengths:
 	
Reading Weaknesses:
		❏ Accommodate the student (circle):
		  o read aloud
		  o reading buddy
		  o recorded text
		  o screen reader
		  o adequate time to finish
		  o critical information highlighted
		  o vocabulary preview
		  o text provided in advance
		  o assignments broken down
		  o quiet place
		❏ Adapt the lesson:

Student Characteristics	Obstacles to Success	Accommodations/Adaptations Needed for Success

Memory Strengths:
 	
Memory Weaknesses:
		❏ Accommodate the student (circle):
		  o multiple intelligences/multisensory approach to instruction
		  o whole-to-part instruction
		  o focus on concepts vs. facts
		  o connect with prior knowledge
		  o real-world connections
		  o advance organizers
		  o preview for instructional units
		  o concept maps
		  o mnemonics
		  o visual imagery
		  o visual or verbal cues and prompts
		  o notes
		  o outlines
		  o formula cards
		  o picture vocabulary
		  o word banks
		  o reteach and review
		  o graphic organizer
		  o study guides
		  o guided practice
		❏ Adapt the lesson:

Tools 71–78: Planning Tools

Tools 71–78: Planning Tools

Student Characteristics	Obstacles to Success	Accommodations/Adaptations Needed for Success

Social/ Emotional Strengths:
 	
Social/ Emotional Weaknesses:
		❏ Accommodate the student (circle):
		   ○ engaging assignments
		   ○ multisensory instruction
		   ○ multiple intelligences incorporated into the classroom
		   ○ flexibility
		   ○ support
		   ○ choices
		   ○ communication
		   ○ positive feedback
		   ○ respect
		   ○ encouragement
		   ○ reasonable/reduced workload
		   ○ feedback
		   ○ success
		   ○ fresh starts
		   ○ lesson connected to student interests
		   ○ humor
		   ○ awareness/acceptance of strengths and needs
		   ○ positive feedback
		❏ Adapt the lesson:

Tool 73: Unit Planning With MI in Mind

Teacher(s): _____

Subject: _____ Unit: _____

Core Content/Objectives for This Unit: _____

Intelligence Area	Curricular Examples	My Ideas for Unit
Verbal-Linguistic Discuss "big" questions, tell stories, or play with words.	• English: What influences people to change their beliefs or actions? • Social Studies: Read/listen to a short biography and tell what you learned in small groups. • Science: Discuss in groups, "What is the most important organ in the human body?" • Math: Listen to the teacher share about the life of a famous mathematician.	
Logical-Mathematical Analyze statistics, numbers, and quantities related to the topic.	• English: Analyze the number of miles traveled by Odysseus. • Social Studies: Analyze poll/census data. • Science: Measure the amount of chlorine in the water. • Math: Determine multiple ways to solve a challenge problem.	

Tools 71–78: Planning Tools

Intelligence Area	Curricular Examples	My Ideas for Unit
Visual-Spatial Analyze, create, and respond to visual representations.	• English: Interpret a painting with a theme or subject related to the novel. • Social Studies: Study a picture or photograph from the period/culture/country. • Science: View a video clip demonstration. • Math: Interpret a chart/graph/table.	
Bodily-Kinesthetic Do something hands-on or physical.	• English: Perform a role-play or brief skit. • Social Studies: Reenact a moment in history. • Science: Conduct an experiment or take a field trip. • Math: Form the shape of a linear equation as a class.	
Musical Analyze, create, and respond to music.	• English: Listen to music from the time period of the novel or use music to introduce mood/tone. • Social Studies: Listen to music from the era being studied. • Science: Listen for patterns in music. • Math: Analyze rhythm and pattern in a piece of music.	

Intelligence Area	Curricular Examples	My Ideas for Unit
Interpersonal Do something with a group.	• English: Conduct a shared-inquiry discussion or group research project. • Social Studies: Take on the roles of members of Congress to debate an issue. • Science: Brainstorm solutions for an open-ended problem with a group. • Math: Work together to determine multiple ways to solve a new kind of math problem.	
Intrapersonal Set goals, reflect, plan, and think.	• English: Reflect on personal beliefs related to the unit. • Social Studies: Determine personal goals for learning about an historical event or concept—why do I care? • Science: Consider a controversial issue related to the unit and prepare a position statement. • Math: Identify three ways in which you will need to use the math concepts from this unit in your personal life or future career.	

Tool 74: Differentiated Lesson Planning Template

Identify Mastery Objectives: What should the students know, understand, or be able to do?

Think About Your Students: Will you differentiate the lesson based on readiness, interests, or learning profiles? How will you collect necessary data in order to group students? How many groups are necessary?

Activator: What will be the common launch experience for the whole class?

Differentiated Process/Instructional Activities:
Group 1:

Group 2:

Group 3:

Differentiated Products/Assessment:
Group 1:

Group 2:

Group 3:

Closure/Summarizer: How will you conclude the learning experience and close the lesson?

Tool 75: Differentiation Pyramid

Directions: The pyramid is a conceptual look at differentiating activities within the classroom. You can record content, process, or product ideas. Use the blank template as you plan for the students in your class.

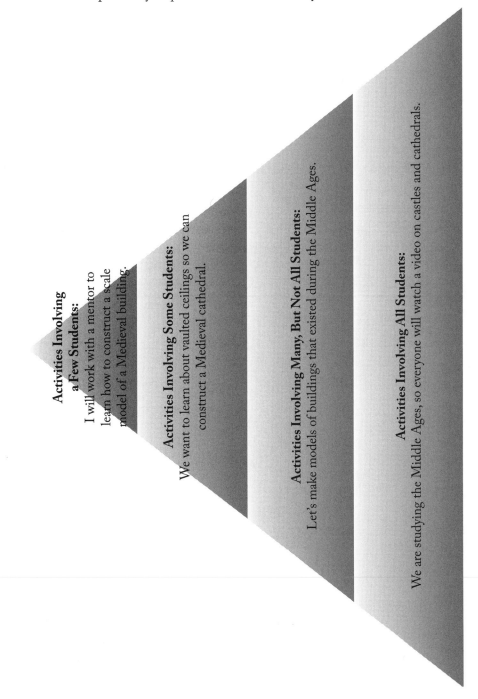

Activities Involving a Few Students:
I will work with a mentor to learn how to construct a scale model of a Medieval building.

Activities Involving Some Students:
We want to learn about vaulted ceilings so we can construct a Medieval cathedral.

Activities Involving Many, But Not All Students:
Let's make models of buildings that existed during the Middle Ages.

Activities Involving All Students:
We are studying the Middle Ages, so everyone will watch a video on castles and cathedrals.

Tools 71–78: Planning Tools

Tools 71–78: Planning Tools

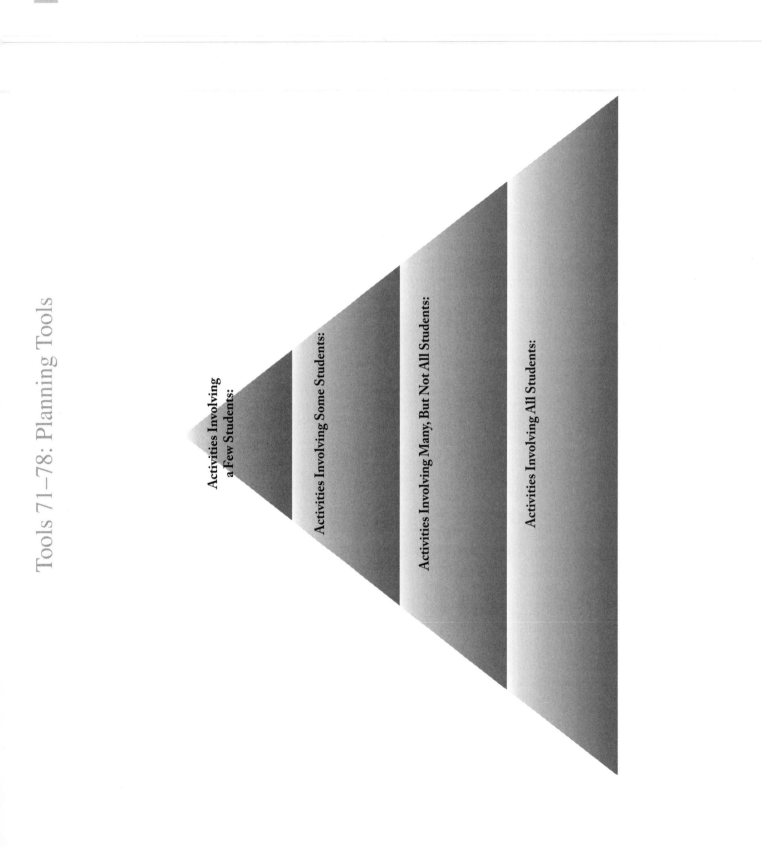

Activities Involving a Few Students:

Activities Involving Some Students:

Activities Involving Many, But Not All Students:

Activities Involving All Students:

Tool 76: Student Tool
Instead of . . . Can I . . . ?

Directions: The next time your teacher gives you an assignment that makes you cringe, use this tool to develop and propose other ways for you to show what you know. Use the ideas from Tool 9 as possible alternatives. Consider the examples and then develop your proposal in the box at the bottom of the chart!

Instead of . . .	Can I . . .
writing a paragraph or an essay	create a PowerPoint presentation?
answering questions from the textbook	highlight important ideas and tell you what I learned?
copying definitions from the dictionary and writing sentences with new vocabulary words	make flashcards with pictures (drawn or clip art) that illustrate the meanings?
memorizing the important dates	create a timeline and verbally explain the sequence and effect of important events?
summarizing the book in writing	create a comic book summary of the book?
Instead of . . .	**Can I . . .**

Tool 77: Assistive Technology Options

Directions: Consider the needs of your student as you plan for his success within a lesson or unit. Select tools that will level the playing field and allow the student to fully access information and demonstrate knowledge.

Student Characteristics	Software Capabilities	Software to Consider
Strong listening comprehension; poor decoding, reading fluency, study, and writing skills.	Scanning/reading software reads text aloud to the student. Study and writing tools sometimes are also embedded.	Screen readers (e.g., Kurzweil 3000, ReadPlease, NaturalReader)
Strong vocabulary and knows what he wants to say, but has poor spelling skills.	Word prediction provides word choices for the student to select from based on initial letters typed. Will read options to student.	Word prediction (e.g., Co:Writer, WordQ)
Has lots of ideas but lacks organization of ideas; does not fully develop details and support for his ideas; ideas and vocabulary are strong but memory and spelling are poor.	Prewriting/organization allows the student to create or complete graphic organizers, outlines, and/or word banks.	Prewriting software (e.g., Kidspiration, Inspiration, Clicker)
Poor fine motor skills; reluctant writer.	Word processing supports writing composition, revising, and editing.	Word processing (e.g., Microsoft Word)
Strong verbal skills but struggles with writing; can't reflect the full extent of his knowledge on paper.	Voice recognition allows the student to dictate ideas verbally into a microphone and the student's words will appear on the computer screen.	Voice recognition (e.g., Dragon Dictation, SpeakQ)
Strong math reasoning and problem solving; lacks automaticity or recall of math facts.	Calculation device supports math calculation.	Calculator

Tool 78: Unit Planning Template

Teacher: _____

Unit: _____

Content	
Theme What is the theme (e.g., 1940s, rainforests, endangered species)?	*Conceptual Learning* What are the essential concepts and understandings?

Critical Thinking	
Critical Thinking What are the higher level questions and tasks for this unit?	
Differentiation *(Advanced Students)* How will I adjust content and materials for students who are ready for more?	*Interests* How does the unit connect to or develop students' interests?

Process and Product		
Integrate the Arts How are the visual and performing arts incorporated?	*Field Trip(s)*	*Multiple Intelligences* Are all eight areas respected throughout the unit?
	Multisensory How are each of the senses/learning styles addressed?	
Assistive/Instructional Technology How are the teacher and students using technology?	*Long-Term Project(s)*	*Alternative Products* Are there various ways to demonstrate knowledge?

Keeping the Bright Turned On!

- ❏ **What's Up?** Catch up with your students and what is happening in their world outside of school. Set aside a time when they can share what's going on with you. Incorporate their interests into your instruction when possible.

- ❏ **The Sweet Taste of Success!** For a variation of the Jar Joys from the earlier chapter, put a token or piece of candy in a jar to represent a student's success in an area (can be general or a predetermined area of focus). Keep the jar on the desk as a constant reminder! After a certain goal is met, tokens can be traded in for rewards or the candy can be taken home.

- ❏ **Portfolio.** Have students review their portfolio periodically to select a favorite piece of work. Compile the favorite works into a class book. Create books throughout the year, perhaps per report period.

- ❏ **Who Cares?!** Students are motivated when they care about a certain topic. Capitalize on this by providing them forums to express themselves through their strengths. Have them draw on their community of learners to create class newspapers, magazines, posters, debates, skits, songs, or videos about the topic of interest. Have the students determine their appropriate audience—who would be interested in hearing about it?

- ❏ **My Space.** Often a pleasing working space helps with organization. Help students design and create a space for school and home that would be conducive to their learning. Provide suggestions and materials (e.g., cardboard to create a personal study carrel, containers for supplies) to help them get organized. Although you can offer suggestions, it often takes time for students to experiment with what works for them.

chapter 5

How Do I Keep the Bright Turned On?

Apply yourself. Get all the education you can, but then . . . do something.
Don't just stand there, make it happen.

—Lee Iacocca

Guiding Questions

❑ How do I share what I have learned with others on behalf of my students?

❑ How do I successfully advocate on behalf of my students?

❑ How do I ensure that my students develop the self-advocacy skills necessary for independence and success in the future?

❑ How do I help my students learn and practice important life skills?

❑ How do I help my students keep the bright turned on?

Word Sparks

✓ advocacy
✓ self-advocacy
✓ self-determination
✓ action plan
✓ goal setting

✓ successful learner
✓ social/emotional
✓ resources
✓ life skills

Chapter Overview

NOW that you have worked so hard to "turn on the bright" with individual students, we will turn our focus toward keeping it turned on. This chapter will show you how to pay it forward by sharing your knowledge with others, by advocating on behalf of the student(s), and by developing advocacy skills within the student and parent. In addition to academic and self-advocacy skills, bright students with learning difficulties need certain life skills to help them successfully navigate their school day such as brainstorming, questioning, understanding personal triggers and coping strategies, and role-playing. This chapter will also explore other avenues, such as mentoring, for keeping the bright turned on. The ultimate goal is for students to possess the skills they will need to carry as they travel on their journey through school and into the real world.

Sharing Your Expertise

It often takes more than one person to provide all of the necessary programming components; therefore, a team approach is critical. This is so important because many educators possess expertise in the area of gifted education *or* special education. Yet few truly understand the unique needs of students who are both incredibly bright and face learning challenges.

What happens when the child leaves your room to go to her other classes? If you are a special educator, what happens when your student returns to her general education class? And what happens next year when that student moves on to the next teacher? What often happens is that these students will be happy and successful with one teacher but struggle in another classroom. One teacher sees strengths that others don't see. The next year, the student starts all over with a teacher who wants to do right by her but may not have the tools in his toolkit to know where to begin. As advocates for these students, you have to see beyond your classroom walls and attempt to impact the student's total school experience. By using the tools in this chapter, you can share what you have learned.

Methods for Sharing

Team meetings and planning sessions. With these students, it is critical to work collaboratively as a team to share perspectives, plan for instruction, and develop and implement strategies and services. The student's team potentially consists of the classroom teacher(s), special educator (who is often the case manager), counselor, gifted educator, administrator, school psychologist, and the parent. The team could meet periodically (weekly, monthly, quarterly) to discuss the strengths and needs of the student and to discuss and tweak goals and programming. This team meeting would be a vehicle for you to share what you have learned about the student with other team members and to help build their knowledge base around this population.

Create a student snapshot. As you learn about the student's strengths and weaknesses, learning style and preferences, and the necessary accommodations/supports and strategies that work, compile this information into an at-a-glance profile (See Tool 79) to share with the team and to pass along to next year's teacher. Seek student and parental input in creating the snapshot. Give a copy to the student to carry as a quick reference regarding her accommodations. Update it periodically so that it remains relevant as the student grows and changes.

Electronic communication. What did we do before e-mail? Set up an address book/contact list with all members of the student's team and communicate about day-to-day performance, assignments, concerns, and successes.

Professional development. Perhaps your grade-level team, department, or entire school staff could benefit from learning more about these kinds of students. Talk to your administrator about conducting in-service workshops in your building and use some of the materials from this book to train others. Or, form a study group to read and use the book together over the course of a semester or year, meeting to discuss and compare notes.

Face-to-face articulation and ongoing involvement. Whenever possible, meet with the student's next teacher or school (include the parent and student if possible) to share what you have learned about the student. Although the student may have a document that states his needs such as a 504 Plan or IEP (or a snapshot you have created), there is nothing like a conversation between teachers to bridge the knowledge gap that exists when students are new to a teacher. Go through the snapshot and focus on imparting the strengths and gifts of the student. Tell a few stories that illustrate the personality of the student, show them some work samples, share alternative products that allowed the student to shine, and explain strategies that work for her. Explain the team's communication methods. The next team will tweak the plan, but information about what worked the year before will help to smooth the transition.

Advocacy on Behalf of the Student

There are often competing perspectives and opinions as to what the child needs. Many educators see only the weaknesses, feel these students are not ready for higher level instructional opportunities, and may therefore exclude them due to their limitations. In their desire to create successes for their child, parents will sometimes request an accommodation or a service that will enable rather than empower the child. In their zeal to think about the greater good of the school, sometimes administrators will say that a service, a program, or a method of instruction is just not possible. In these (and many other) circumstances, someone has to step up to be the student's advocate. Parents of these students frequently tell us that they had to "fight" for services for their child and they interpret advocacy as a battle and the school as the battleground. But advocacy is not a fight. The tools in this chapter will help you to pursue purposeful, gentle, and effective advocacy. The goal is for these students to get what they need while preserving harmony on the team and in your building.

Methods for Advocacy

Share your expertise. Sharing and building knowledge on behalf of a student or this population at large is a form of advocacy.

Monitor the student's program. Be aware of the student's total school experience and what's going on in other settings throughout her day. Communicate with other staff members involved in the student's education, talk to the student about what is happening in her other classes and groups, and talk to the parents about what they see. If you see yourself in the role of advocate for this student (regardless of your actual role—be it special educator, general educator, speech pathologist, or counselor) it is your business to know what is going on. Let people know that you plan to be involved in positive ways on behalf of the student.

Create an intervention plan. Take time to look at a student's current and future educational programming. How will you lay the groundwork that will get him where he needs to go (e.g., advanced coursework, positive self-concept)? Make a specific plan that details actions, a timeline, and persons responsible. This way, everyone is on the same page about the vision for the student and how to get there.

Speak up. Many times, the best-intentioned teachers do not feel empowered to change things for students outside of their own classroom. But if you see a decision being made that just isn't right, then something needs to be said. For example, if a student like Darryl was being kept in for recess every day because he did not finish his assignments in writing class—speak up. If a student like Jeremy was being punished for being "rude" to the PE teacher and his classmates—speak up. If a student like Sarah was not placed in the advanced math class because the teacher felt she couldn't keep up with the workload— speak up. It takes a strong person to express an opinion that contrasts with that of a colleague, but your opinion is backed by knowledge and research on what works for this population; you are not arguing—you are sharing your expertise.

Form a committee. Speak to your administrator about the need for a twice-exceptional committee and the positive impact that it would have on your school's performance as a whole. Find others who have the best interests of students in mind and attempt to have a variety of disciplines and roles represented (e.g., general educators, special educators, occupational therapists, speech pathologists, counselor, school psychologist, GT teacher). Use this committee as a vehicle for appropriately recognizing, identifying, and serving this population in your building. Use identified students as the catalyst for change within your building.

Get to know your administrator. Be seen as someone who actively works to support the school. Be involved in committees, take on extra responsibilities, and be a positive contributor at staff meetings and professional development sessions. Then, when you need to advocate on behalf of a student, be prepared to share the research base that supports your recommendation and explain how the recommendation will directly affect student achievement. Together you can come up with a solution that works for the student and for the school.

Advocate for gifted programming. Look for existing opportunities for the student to be in challenging classes and groups and recommend that the student be placed in those opportunities. Be prepared to share the strengths of the student that make this opportunity a match for her and also be ready to explain how you will support her areas of weakness. This might be by volunteering to meet with the teacher to discuss the student's necessary accommodations and how to implement them. It might be by supporting the student with her assignments and projects directly or via communication with her parents. One reason some educators are reluctant to include these students in their advanced classes and groups is that they fear that they will not be able to support them adequately. Provide initial support and reassurance to the teachers. If your district has special magnet or gifted programs, encourage the student and parent to apply and submit a letter of recommendation if you feel it is a good match for the student. Many students who are bored with on-level curriculum will light up and begin to reach their academic potential when they are appropriately challenged.

Advocate for accommodations and special services. If you feel the student needs more than informal supports and accommodations in order to access the curriculum at the appropriate level in light of his intellect, you should initiate the formal processes in place in your district for determining eligibility for a 504 Plan or an IEP. Most often the first step is to identify the specific areas of concern (e.g., reading decoding or fluency, attention/organization). Using the Response to Intervention methodology espoused by most states, determine the student's baseline performance in the area(s) of concern and develop appropriate interventions to address the problem area. As a team, set goals for expected progress that are appropriate in light of the student's ability. Minute, incremental progress should not be considered sufficient. Keep data and if the student does not respond, or needs such a huge amount of support in order to respond that it approximates special education support or cannot be sustained due to limited resources, your data may make the case for you. Then speak up.

Advocacy (backed by data) from an empowered classroom teacher often documents the need for formal services. This also applies to situations where the services in place are inadequate or where other, related services (e.g., speech/language, occupational therapy, counseling) may also be needed.

Support parent advocacy efforts. Many parents are positive and effective advocates for their child. They know what their child needs and they figure out how to navigate the educational system in order to get it. They may have the financial ability to pay for private evaluations and come to the school team with helpful information and a firm dedication to obtaining appropriate services for their child. Some parents may not have the resources, the knowledge, or the comfort level required to push the issue and so they must rely on the school to know what's best. Help these families by sharing the Parent Partnership Pieces in this book as well as resources where they can learn more about their child's needs and the way your school system operates. Many parents don't know that if they request an IEP evaluation for their child then the school team will meet to review data and make a determination about eligibility for services. Let parents know this information and that they have your ear and your support.

Teaching Self-Advocacy

If we truly want the student to become an independent, successful learner who is ready for college and beyond, we must pass the torch to him or her. In our experience, the predictors for success in high school and beyond for these students are a positive self-concept and strong self-advocacy skills. A high school student could read or write at the elementary level and still be successful in Advanced Placement classes if he sees himself as a capable learner (self-concept) and is comfortable requesting and utilizing accommodations that allow him to access the course material and to demonstrate his knowledge. A student with ADHD who reads at a college level can fail that same AP course if she does not view herself as a competent student and is embarrassed or unskilled at asking for and accepting help.

Stages for Self-Advocacy Development

Develop self-awareness. We have found that many teachers just expect these students to be self-advocates. They are smart so they should be able to ask for their accommodations and tell their teachers what they need. But often these kids feel a range of emotions (e.g., frustration, anger, worry, sadness) related to their school experience that inhibits their development of a positive self-concept, making them feel stuck. They often do not know the nature of their gifts and disabilities; they do not understand why they feel stupid when everyone keeps telling them they are smart. It just doesn't make sense. The path to teaching self-advocacy begins with helping students to understand their strengths and weaknesses and (in age-appropriate ways) to begin to understand the nature of their difficulties.

Encourage self-acceptance. Once the students know who they are, they can begin to learn to accept this in positive ways. Students often heave a sigh of relief when they find out there is a name (e.g., LD, ADHD, Asperger's) for their difficulties and that others experience them as well. When they meet other smart kids with similar learning difficulties or learn about famous people with difficulties who are successful, then they feel they finally have a place in this world and it's not such a bad place after all.

Promote self-determination. The next step is to have students set realistic goals for themselves and to become involved in decision making regarding their schooling. At this point, many students are ready to participate (in age-appropriate ways) in their own IEP and 504 Plan meetings to help the team determine which supports would work best for them. They may be ready to sit with their parent as e-mails to and from teachers are written and read. They are invested in what is important to them and take steps to achieve their personal goals. Be forewarned: They do not always have the same personal goals that their teacher or parents have for them, but it is critical to incorporate students' feedback into plans and decisions or you will lose their support. Students at this stage need to see their burgeoning self-advocacy efforts working or they will give up and buy out of the process. If they say they don't like using the new organization system, take time to find out why and to incorporate their feedback into tweaking it.

Cultivate self-advocacy. The students are now ready to act on their own behalf and to speak up for themselves and their needs. They should feel a sense of control over their own destiny and have important goals driving them to succeed. It is important to teach them how to ask appropriately for what they need and to access resources. At this point they are probably speaking more in meetings and writing more e-mails than their parents. Know that you can't start at this stage if a student hasn't progressed through the previous stages. It can't be forced, so regardless of their age, start where they are and take the necessary steps to move them forward.

Student Profiles

Sarah

During her fifth-grade year, Sarah's homeroom teacher began to be concerned. The school team had created an environment where she was meeting with academic and social success on a daily basis. But she was very dependent on the adults and the environment for that success. If there was a substitute who didn't know Sarah, she had an "off day." The team members knew that they needed to educate the middle school teachers about her so that they could continue the positive work with Sarah. They set a date for an articulation meeting over the summer. They also knew that they had to begin working on Sarah's self-advocacy so that she could create her own success. Because Sarah had been experiencing a lot of success, her self-esteem wasn't bad, but she didn't feel great about herself either. She didn't really understand why the teachers had to help her so much and why she had such a difficult time with writing and organization. The team crafted a plan for developing Sarah's self-advocacy using the tools provided in this book, starting with self-awareness. Sarah's self-concept bloomed and by the end of the year she was beginning to request some of her accommodations and attend her IEP meeting as an active participant.

Jeremy

During his sixth-grade year, Jeremy was a puzzle to most of his teachers. They hadn't worked with a student like him before and didn't know how to handle his quirky behaviors and social difficulties. He was having a lot of trouble transitioning from the nurturing elementary school setting and was having frequent meltdowns. Jeremy's special educator had recently read this book and other resources for students with Asperger's syndrome and she knew she had to intervene. The team agreed they needed help so they decided to meet weekly after school to discuss Jeremy. The special educator shared information and resources with them about Asperger's, and the team even invited his fifth-grade team to come and talk about Jeremy and what worked for them. They reviewed research-based best practices and strategies and decided as a team which to implement. With his parents' input, they put in place predictable routines and consistent structures and developed a behavior plan for Jeremy. Slowly and steadily, Jeremy's performance began to improve.

Darryl

Darryl was one of those bubbly, happy kids who seemed unaffected by his disability at first. His parents were nurturing and loving and he had a lot of friends. He seemed so bright that the school team wasn't concerned about him. They figured his reading and writing would come along; after all, students develop at different stages. Meanwhile, Darryl began falling further and further behind, and his third-grade classroom teacher was concerned. She had just finished reading this book and knew that despite her efforts and commitment to his success, Darryl needed something more than she could provide if he was to reach his true potential. She followed the tips for advocating on behalf of Darryl and was able to convince the team and Darryl's parents that he truly needed IEP services. With these supports, Darryl has been able to demonstrate his gifts and to achieve at high levels.

Conclusion

Now that you have an understanding of what it takes to keep the bright turned on, you are ready to use the tools in this chapter. Beyond making your classroom an environment that is conducive to success for the student, it is important to teach the student how to advocate for himself. This way, he will be able to successfully navigate all other learning environments, now and in the future, even if the best practices are not in place. You will be able to create action plans, provide opportunities for advocacy, and give your students tools to continue their quest to be successful, lifelong learners.

Tool 79:
Student Profile: At-A-Glance

Condensing information into an easy-to-read and easy-to-use format can be an effective and efficient way to share information about the student or transfer information during the articulation process, helping to ensure that the bright is kept turned on.

Tips

✓ *Tool 79: Student Profile: At-A-Glance.* Use this tool to create a "student snapshot." It can be used as an updated profile for a student to carry in his or her notebook; as an aid for parent-teacher conferencing; as a capture sheet for next year's teacher; as a capture sheet for meetings with other staff members; as a tool for communicating with doctors and other support personnel working with the child and family; and for any other purpose that will help you help your student.

Tool 79: Student Profile: At-A-Glance

Name: _____

Strengths	Interests

Needs, Obstacles, Stumbling Blocks

Learning Style

Important Data and Instruments Used

Tool 79: Student Profile: At-A-Glance

Adaptations/Accommodations	Interventions

Instructional Strategies

What Works	Other

Tools 80–86:
Self-Advocacy

Self-advocacy is the ability to communicate effectively about who you are and what you need. Learning and practicing strategies for developing self-advocacy make it possible for these students to become risk-takers and lifelong learners. Over time, students develop the skills and maturity that allow them to become partners in decision making.

Tips

✓ *Tool 80: Self-Advocacy Discussion Starters.* These questions and definitions are a great way to introduce topics related to self-advocacy in one-on-one or small-group discussions. Grouping bright students with learning difficulties together for these conversations is recommended, as they often share common experiences and feelings.

✓ *Tool 81: Student Tool: What Defines Me As a Successful Learner?* Use this tool to conference with students to help them identify their strengths and needs. Encourage students to share the information with their other teachers. Provide opportunities for students to role-play as a way to practice self-advocacy, so that they are comfortable sharing what they need to succeed.

✓ *Tool 82: Student Tool: My Talent Pool.* As a first step in goal setting, have students reflect on where they are now, the talents they already have, and the ones they may want to develop.

✓ *Tool 83: Student Tool: Goal Setting.* To be able to set goals, it is important to understand different types of goals. Use this tool to help students set personal goals, create a plan, implement the plan, and evaluate their progress toward the goal.

✓ *Tool 84: Student Tool: If It Is to Be, It's Up to Me!* Knowing what you want is an important precursor to self-advocacy. This tool will guide students to see beyond the present and set personal goals for where they want to be in the future.

✓ *Tool 85: Student Tool: How I See Myself.* Students visualize themselves in the future and draw pictures to illustrate their hopes and dreams.

✓ *Tool 86: Student Tool: Student Letter to Teacher.* Use this tool to help your students write a letter to their next teacher that will share what they have learned about themselves and what they need to be successful.

Tools 80–86: Self-Advocacy

Tools 80–86: Self-Advocacy

Tool 80: Self-Advocacy Discussion Starters

Self-Awareness: Having knowledge about yourself and your disability.
   Discussion Questions:
   - What is your learning style?
   - What are your interests?
   - What do you value?
   - What are your strengths (academic, behavioral, social)? Weaknesses?
   - What is your disability? What does that mean for you?
   - What kinds of supports do you require? What accommodations do you prefer?

Self-Acceptance: Being okay with yourself just the way you are.
   Discussion Questions:
   - Are you comfortable with yourself the way you are? What do you like about you? What do you wish was different? If you were different, would you still be you?
   - Do you accept your personal strengths and weaknesses?
   - Can you accept help when teachers or others offer it to you?

Self-Determination: Setting goals and making decisions about what is best for you, based on your knowledge of yourself, and being willing to take risks to achieve these goals.
   Discussion Questions:
   - What is important to you?
   - What are your personal and academic goals?
   - What actions do you need to take to reach your goals?
   - How will you know when you have reached your goals?
   - How hard are you willing to work to reach your goals?

Self-Advocacy: Acting on your own behalf; speaking up for yourself and your needs clearly and directly and with confidence.
   Discussion Questions:
   - Are you in control of your life and your choices?
   - Do you know how to ask for what you need?
   - Do you know how to access support/resources? Have you done so?
   - Do you attend your IEP/504 Plan meetings? Do you give input on developing your IEP/504 Plan?

Tool 81: Student Tool
What Defines Me As a Successful Learner?

Who I am! (strengths and needs)

_____

_____

_____

_____

What I need! (adaptations and accommodations)

_____

_____

_____

_____

Which tools work for me? (interventions and strategies)

_____

_____

_____

_____

How to get what I need to succeed!

_____

_____

_____

_____

Tools 80–86: Self-Advocacy

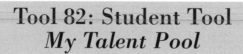

Tool 82: Student Tool
My Talent Pool

Directions: What are some talents that you have or that you wish to develop? Write or draw them below.

Tool 83: Student Tool
Goal Setting

Directions: In the template below, identify your personal goals in each category.

Very Short-Term Goals are those we set for the very near future—today, tomorrow, next week.
Examples: daily, weekly completion of assignments; doing well on a test; raising my hand and taking turns; helping a classmate
My very short-term goals:
Short-Term Goals are those we set for the near future—week, weeks, month or two.
Examples: weekly progress in learning math facts; being better organized; completing a long-term assignment; inviting a friend over to play
My short-term goals:

Tools 80–86: Self-Advocacy

Long-Term Goals are those we set for the more distant future—grading period, semester.

Examples: raising grades from one marking period to the next

My long-term goals:

Very Long-Term Goals are those we set for very far off in the future—year, middle school, high school, postsecondary school.

Examples: taking honors and/or AP courses; applying for special programs like magnet schools; arranging internships and community service projects

My very long-term goals:

Life Goals are those we set to live our life by into adulthood—college, career path, graduate school, serving the community.

Examples: making meaningful and lasting personal and professional relationships

My life goals:

Tool 84: Student Tool
If It Is to Be, It's Up to Me!

Something I really want to happen is . . .

Things I have to do to get what I want include . . .

Help that I need to get what I want . . .

My plan to get what I want . . .

What Will I Do?	When Will I Do It?

Tools 80–86: Self-Advocacy

Tool 85: Student Tool
How I See Myself

Next year

In 3 years

Tools 80–86: Self-Advocacy

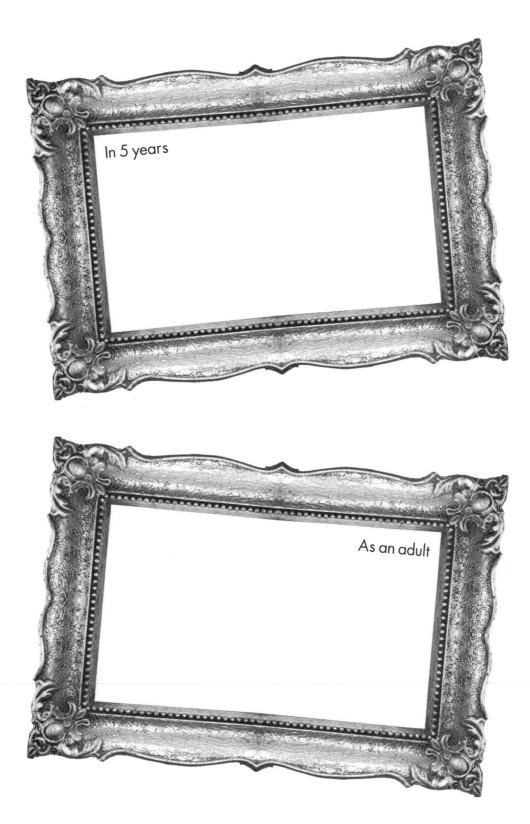

In 5 years

As an adult

Tool 86: Student Tool
Student Letter to Teacher

Directions: You have worked hard this year and have learned a lot about your strengths and about what you need to be successful. Next year you will have a new teacher. Tell your teacher all about yourself so that he or she will be able to make sure you continue to be successful. Fill in the spaces below as a graphic organizer for your ideas. Then, use another piece of paper (or a computer) to write a letter to your new teacher.

Things I'm good at

Things that are hard for me

Interesting things about me

Tools 80–86: Self-Advocacy

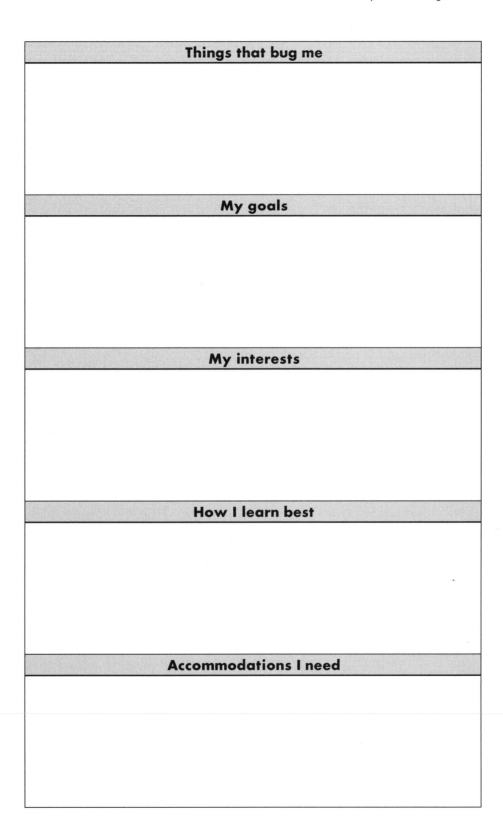

Things that bug me

My goals

My interests

How I learn best

Accommodations I need

Tools 80–86: Self-Advocacy

Tools 87–92:
Life Skills for Learning

Often these students have trouble with their interpersonal skills or keeping their emotions in check. Little issues that crop up throughout the school day become obstacles to learning that can be just as significant as reading or writing difficulties. Therefore, these students need certain life skills to help them work through real-time problems and issues and to successfully navigate their school day (see Barnes-Robinson & Jeweler, 2007, for ideas and information). Such skills not only contribute to the student's ability to be an effective self-advocate but also impact his or her success, both in and out of school.

Tips

✓ *Tool 87: Brainstorming.* Brainstorming provides the student with the opportunity to share her ideas without the fear of being judged or criticized. It encourages flexibility, as well as creative and critical thinking.

✓ *Tool 88: Student Tool: Active Listening.* The better you are at listening, the better you are at brainstorming and questioning, which in turn makes you a better problem solver. This skill can help students both socially and academically, because as good listeners, they become more aware of others and the world around them.

✓ *Tool 89: Student Tool: Triggers.* This activity helps students improve their relationships with peers and adults by learning to be more mindful of when their buttons have been pushed and when they have pushed the buttons of others. They will learn about the warning signs of trouble and how they can control their responses to create a more positive outcome (Zimmer, 1998).

✓ *Tool 90: Top 10 Triggers* and *Top 10 Coping Mechanisms.* Use this tool with students to remind them of what things trigger them and their classmates and to discuss possible coping strategies that they can use. You can use the suggestions here to have your students make posters for the classroom with their own triggers and coping mechanisms.

✓ *Tool 91: Student Tool: Questioning.* Asking questions opens dialogue, focuses thinking, helps people make connections, and encourages creative solutions. Some questions give us limited information, while others encourage new and original ideas and help develop new information. In the Question Quest activity, have students use the question starters or matrix to develop questions about the problem and then discuss them. Teachers initially should help students to write good questions that will help them solve the problem in positive ways.

✓ *Tool 92: Role-Playing.* Role-plays give kids a way to practice what they are learning in real-life scenarios. They give teachers and parents a structured process to help students improve their communication and self-advocacy skills. Using this strategy can help make kids more comfortable and confident when implementing a new skill. It also helps them to learn and practice appropriate ways to interact with adults and peers.

Tools 87–92: Life Skills for Learning

Tool 87: Brainstorming

Directions: Brainstorming is a great way to come up with a lot of ideas for solving a problem. When many ideas are generated, there are more opportunities to pick the best one when solving a problem. Therefore, accepting all ideas without judgment is an important part of brainstorming. Follow these steps to brainstorm solutions to a problem as a class:

1. On the board or scratch paper, have students brainstorm problems that kids regularly face at school. (Possible problems may include teasing and bullying in the locker room, getting a bad grade you don't think you deserve, a fight with a friend in the lunch room, or your homework is always lost/late.)

2. As a group, have students brainstorm possible solutions to *one* of those problems.

3. Have your students come up with criteria to judge their solutions. Based on their criteria, have them identify the solutions that would be the best to use. A great next step would be to have the students role-play a scenario using their solutions.

Tool 88: Student Tool
Active Listening

Active listening is the process of hearing what is being said and understanding the message that is being sent. It means making eye contact, acknowledging what is said, and being able to paraphrase back to the speaker the content of the message and the feelings behind the message. It is very important to communicate our understandings of each other's thoughts and feelings. How can we tell if someone is really listening to what we are saying? Here are some ways a good listener behaves:

Verbal	**Nonverbal**
Asks questions	Nods head
Summarizes for understanding	Makes eye contact
Speaks respectfully	Faces the speaker
Makes suggestions	Smiles

Make a list of other verbal indicators of good listening.

_____

_____

_____

_____

Make a list of other nonverbal indicators of good listening.

_____

_____

_____

_____

With a partner, take turns discussing your dreams for the future. First, use poor listening behaviors and then use active listening behaviors. Talk about how you felt as the speaker when your partner used each of the listening behaviors.

Tools 87–92: Life Skills for Learning

Tool 89: Student Tool
Triggers

Triggers are things that cause us to become upset. Triggers are both verbal (words) and nonverbal (actions) stimuli that cause us to react negatively out of anger or frustration.

- ❑ **Warning Signs:** How do you know when you are feeling angry or upset? Do you breathe faster, turn red, sweat, or clench a fist? Recognizing your warning signs can help you avoid problems.
- ❑ **Coping Strategies:** Now, what should you do when you start to feel frustrated or angry? Using coping strategies (such as counting to 10 or taking deep breaths) can help you to feel better, so that you make good choices and stay out of trouble.

Directions: Answer the questions below to help you understand and learn about your triggers.

My Triggers

What words upset me?

_____

_____

_____

What actions upset me (at school or at home)?

_____

_____

_____

My Warning Signs

What happens to my body when I am upset?

_____

_____

_____

What do I think and feel when I am upset?

_____

_____

_____

How can I tell when someone else is upset?

_____

_____

_____

Coping Mechanisms

What do I do with my body to show other people that I am in control when I am angry or upset?

_____

_____

_____

What do I say to show others that I am in control when I am angry or upset?

_____

_____

_____

Do I get upset quickly or slowly? Is one better than the other?

_____

_____

_____

Brainstorm strategies that help you and others to cope with frustration and angry feelings.

_____

_____

_____

Tool 90: Top 10 Triggers and Top 10 Coping Mechanisms

Things That Bug Me:

1. Eye rolling
2. Fist raising
3. Snubbing
4. Tapping pencil on desk
5. Name calling
6. Interrupting
7. Shouting down
8. Teasing
9. Laughing in your face
10. Getting a bad grade

Things That De-Bug Me:

1. Counting to 10.
2. Walking away.
3. Listening to music.
4. Doing something physical (such as punching a pillow, going for a run, squeezing a stress ball).
5. Taking deep breaths.
6. Talking to the teacher or a friend about the problem.
7. Giving myself a pep talk.
8. Ignoring the situation/person causing my frustration.
9. Getting a drink of water.
10. Going to a quiet area.

Tool 91: Student Tool
Questioning

Directions: In the Question Quest activity, each team will choose a problem or conflict that you are facing in school and write it on the line below. Take turns creating a question about the problem by using a word from the top row and the left column. Write the question below the grid and record your team name in the appropriate square on the grid. Now no one else can use that square! After you have finished the whole grid or run out of the time given by your teacher, count up the points each team has earned and determine the winner! Then, discuss the different kinds of questions asked and which gave you the best information to solve the problem.

Sample Problem: Kids are teasing me when I get help with reading in class.

Sample Questions: Why might the kids be teasing me? Why should I get so upset? Who can help me solve this problem?

Problem or Situation: _____

	Is/Isn't	Do/Does	Might/ Might Not	Would/ Wouldn't	Should/ Shouldn't	Can/ Can't
Who	1 point	1 point	1 point	2 points	2 points	2 points
What	1 point	1 point	1 point	2 points	2 points	2 points
When/ Where	1 point	1 point	1 point	2 points	2 points	2 points
Which	2 points	2 points	2 points	3 points	3 points	3 points
Why	2 points	2 points	2 points	3 points	3 points	3 points
How/ What If	2 points	2 points	2 points	3 points	3 points	3 points

Questions: _____

_____

_____

Team # 1 Points: _____ **Team #2 Points:** _____

Tool 92: Role-Playing

Directions: Role-playing helps students practice interactions that are hard for them. Select a scenario from the cards below (or develop one using actual problems that your students are having). Make copies of each task card for the students. Read the scenario with them. Identify a role for each student by circling it on his or her card. Give students time to think about and plan what they are going to say. Have students act out the scenarios then reflect on the role-play experience. Debrief by discussing how role-playing can help when handling a problem.

The Dog Ate It!

Roles: Natalie, Teacher, Mother

Scenario: Natalie does her homework but forgets to turn it in. Her teacher calls Natalie's mother to tell her she is not doing her homework. Natalie's mother is positive that Natalie has done her homework because she checks it.

Task: What should Natalie do?

Your Notes/Plan:

Hey, Stupid!

Roles: Tim, Darcy, Bus Driver

Scenario: Two kids, Tim and Darcy, are standing at the bus stop. The bus comes and Darcy steps in front of Tim in line. Tim is so angry that he thinks to himself, "Hey, stupid, I was here first."

Task: What should Tim do?

Your Notes/Plan:

That's Not Fair!

Roles: Sam, Teacher

Scenario: When passing out the test papers, the teacher said, "Some of you lost points for not showing all of your work." Sam was angry when he received his math test back because he lost points on almost every question for not showing his work. Every answer was correct, but his grade was a C instead of an A. He was so mad that he wanted to rip up the test and leave the room.

Task: What should Sam do?

Your Notes/Plan:

Tools 93–99:
The Magic of Mentoring

A mentor program may be one of the most powerful tools at your fingertips and one of the easiest to implement. Giving students the opportunity to work one-on-one with a mentor provides an optimal match and ideal climate for gifted students with learning difficulties to become aware of their potential and shine! This section provides information on how to develop a mentor program at your school. It is based on the WINGS Mentor Program (Shevitz, Weinfeld, Jeweler, & Barnes-Robinson, 2003), developed in Montgomery County Public Schools, MD, which has been positively impacting students for 20 years (see http://www.montgomeryschoolsmd.org/curriculum/enriched/mcpsprograms/wings/index.shtm).

Tips

- ✓ *Tool 93: Principles of an Effective Mentor Program.* These principles have proven to be the basis of a successful mentor program.
- ✓ *Tool 94: The Mentor Process.* Use these suggestions to develop your own mentor program.
- ✓ *Tool 95: Student Interview for Mentor Program.* Use these questions to help you match a mentor to your student. Consider student interest areas, personalities of the mentor and student, and how well the mentor's style matches the student to be mentored.
- ✓ *Tool 96: Mentor Training.* It is important your mentors be trained on the characteristics of bright students with learning difficulties, what works and what doesn't, mentoring principles and best practices, and the role of the mentor.
- ✓ *Tool 97: Student Tool: What I Learned About Myself.* Provide the student with the opportunity to reflect on the mentor process either alone or with the mentor.
- ✓ *Tool 98: Student Tool: Project Ideas.* Help students record their ideas for future projects and encourage them to continue pursuing their interests and passions.
- ✓ *Tool 99: Parent Partnership Piece: Keeping the Bright Turned On!* This is a culminating piece that helps parents keep their children engaged in learning.

Tool 93: Principles of an Effective Mentor Program

You can develop a mentor program in your school by seeking volunteers either within your school, among your parents, or in the community to work with certain students in your class.

1. *Focus on strengths and interests*: Attention is directed to a student's strengths, interests, and potential for success. Give a student the chance to delve in depth in a topic of her own interest and the student will become actively engaged in her own learning.

2. *Build on success*: Find a mentor who nurtures the student's gifts and talents and validates her as a successful learner. The mentor will help the student pursue an exciting topic, while aiding her in developing skills necessary to be successful in school. In addition, the mentor helps the student learn strategies to circumvent her areas of weakness while focusing on her strengths.

3. *Enhance self-esteem*: Through her successes, the student will gain self-confidence, which contributes to increased self-esteem and excitement about learning.

4. *Project-based at its best*: Over the course of the mentoring, the student will develop a project that reflects what she has learned, a natural outlet for allowing for alternative products, enabling her to gain awareness of her capabilities and learning styles.

5. *Student presentations*: Allow time for the student to present her project to her peers and the results will astonish you! The student will receive much positive feedback from her classmates, boosting her self-esteem. The presentation is often the first time that others see the student as smart.

Tool 94: The Mentor Process

The following describes a sample process. You will want to develop a process that will work best in your school setting.

1. Determine the length of the mentor program and a time that the student will meet with the mentor. Allow an adequate length of time to develop the relationship, research the topic in depth, and create an original product (minimum of eight sessions is suggested).

2. Choose a time period that is least disruptive to the student's day. Students should not be required to make up missed work. Decide on the length and frequency of sessions; an hour once a week seems to work well.

3. Find a quiet place for the mentor and student to work.

4. The teacher/coordinator meets with the student to be mentored to explain the program and determine if he is interested in participating. If interested, the teacher/coordinator interviews the student using Tool 95 to determine his areas of passion and interest.

5. Match the mentor and student.

6. Meet with the mentor to share information about the strengths and needs of the student.

7. Provide a process for the mentor to communicate with the teacher. This allows the mentor to have an avenue to share information/successes with the teacher after each session and to use the teacher as a resource if the mentor needs support.

8. By keeping the teacher informed of the mentor sessions, the teacher can then engage in conversation with the student about what he is learning.

9. The mentor meets with the student at the designated time, helping the student explore the student-selected topic in depth and design a project that reflects what is learned. The mentor serves as a guide, nurturing the student's talents and gifts, while providing strategies for circumventing the areas of need.

10. Plan time for the mentors to meet to share their expertise and experiences, exchange ideas, and problem solve. Some of the best ideas come out of these meetings.

11. Provide an opportunity for the students to present their projects to the class or other appropriate audiences.

12. As a culminating activity, hold a Show–Off Night in which the students who participated in the mentor program come together to share their projects and the parents and teachers celebrate their accomplishments (Shevitz et al., 2003).

Tool 95: Student Interview
for Mentor Program

Use the questions below as a springboard for interviewing your student.

1. What do you like to do in your spare time?

_____

_____

2. What do you like about school? What are your favorite subjects (other than lunch and recess)?

_____

_____

3. If you could study anything that you wanted, what would you pick?

_____

_____

4. If you went to the media center for a nonfiction book or turned on the TV to watch an educational show, what might it be about?

_____

_____

5. Do you like to do projects or make things? What kind of projects do you like?

_____

_____

6. What types of things would you be interested in studying with your mentor?

_____

_____

Tools 93–99: The Magic of Mentoring

7. How did you become interested in the topic? How long have you been interested in the topic?

_____

_____

8. What do you already know about the topic?

_____

_____

9. What do you want to find out about the topic?

_____

_____

Tool 96: Mentor Training

Components of the mentor training include:

1. *Teach the characteristics of bright students with learning difficulties.* Mentors need to develop an understanding of who these students are. Reprint the characteristics of these students (Tool 2) and present the information to the mentor. Keep in mind that mentors may not see weaknesses that teachers see and teachers may not see strengths that the mentors see due to the one-on-one nature of the program.

2. *Present the guiding principles of the mentor program.*
   - ❏ Focus on the strengths and interests of the student.
   - ❏ Build on success.
   - ❏ Enhance self-esteem.
   - ❏ Use project-based learning.
   - ❏ Share knowledge with an appropriate audience.

3. *Define the mentor's role.*
   - ❏ Support and guide the student to develop in an area of interest, while developing a caring, respectful relationship with the mentee.
   - ❏ Be a facilitator, allowing the student to lead.
   - ❏ Be positive and recognize the student's accomplishments.
   - ❏ Help the student set realistic goals within the timeframe provided.
   - ❏ Help the mentee organize and plan the long-term project, breaking it down into steps.
   - ❏ Be a good listener. Mentors say that sometimes the most important thing they do is listen to the student.
   - ❏ Validate the student as a learner by your presence and interest in the student and by valuing his interests.

4. *Review the mentor process* (Tool 94).
5. *Share strategies that you have learned that work with these students* (Tool 57).

Tools 93–99: The Magic of Mentoring

Tool 97: Student Tool
What I Learned About Myself

Working with a mentor can teach you a lot of things about yourself and your interests, strengths, and abilities. As you worked with your mentor and planned your project, you may have learned more about your learning style, attitudes, and goals for your future. Take some time to think about your experience with your mentor and record your thoughts below.

While I was working with my mentor, I learned the following about:

My Interests: I enjoy _____

My Strengths and Abilities: I am good at _____

My Learning Style: I work best when I can _____

My New Skills: I learned how to _____

My Goals: In the future I would like to _____

What I Learned About Myself

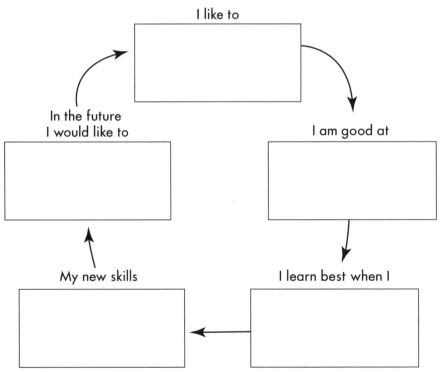

Tool 98: Student Tool
Project Ideas

Topics that I would like to explore in the future

My ideas and projects that I would like to work on

Tool 99: Parent Partnership Piece
Keeping the Bright Turned On!

Dear Parent,

As the year draws to a close, and our journey together to turn on the bright in each child comes to an end, I would like to leave you with one last request—keep the bright turned on! One very simple way that you, as the parent, can accomplish this task is to continue to nurture your child's interests and passions. Take advantage of special programs and events in the area, expose your child to new ideas and topics, and allow him or her to pursue his or her dreams!

In addition to what you do personally with your child, we have found mentoring to be one of the most powerful tools for students. Having an adult who shares your child's interest to help guide his or her study and nurture his or her talents has been shown to be an effective way to validate a student's interests and provide a unique opportunity for the student to see him- or herself as a successful learner. Once you know your child's interests and passions, keep your eyes and ears open for someone who just may be interested in becoming a mentor. It may be someone in your child's school, a friend or relative, or you may find someone through a mutual friend. We have found the relationship that develops between mentor and student is priceless and the impact is immeasurable. By guiding and nurturing your child's interests, the mentor is able to help your child recognize his or her academic and creative potential and see that that there is a niche for him or her in the world.

Wishing you and your family a wonderful summer.

Sincerely,

Tools 100 and 101: Action Plans

Action plans are a great way to determine what needs to be done to bring programming and services for twice-exceptional students closer to the ideal state. The first step is to identify areas of need, pinpointing the gap between the ideal state and the actual or current state. Once this gap has been identified, set realistic and achievable goals that will move you closer to the ideal state. Once those goals are attained, develop a new action plan and start the cycle of growth all over again until you have achieved the desired results!

Tips

✓ *Tool 100: Now What? Planning for Action!* Use the questions in this tool to identify areas of strength and areas where growth is still needed in your classroom or school. Then use Tool 101 to create an action plan for taking services for these students to the next level!

✓ *Tool 101: Action Plan Template.* Use the template to develop and record your plan for improving programming and services for bright students with learning difficulties in your classroom and/or school.

Tool 100: Now What? Planning for Action!

Directions: For each portion of the chart, reflect on your (or your team's) areas of strength and areas where growth is still needed.

Who Are These Kids?	
Guiding Questions: Do I (or we) . . . ❑ Understand the characteristics of bright students with varying difficulties and disabilities? ❑ Recognize the strengths and weaknesses of these students, despite the masks that they may wear? ❑ Understand the social-emotional characteristics and needs of these students?	
Areas of Strength	Areas Where Growth Is Needed

How Do I Find These Kids?	
Guiding Questions: Do I (or we) . . . ❑ Understand the obstacles to identification for these students? ❑ Implement best practices for identification and use appropriate tools for identification? ❑ Appropriately recognize and free potential and unmask their gifts? ❑ Appropriately recognize and unmask these students' learning problems?	
Areas of Strength	Areas Where Growth Is Needed

How Do I Reach Them?

Guiding Questions: Do I (or we)
- ❏ Provide best practices for instruction such as:
    - ▪ Access to rigorous instruction?
    - ▪ Instruction and interventions to address the learning problems?
    - ▪ Appropriate adaptations and accommodations?
    - ▪ Case management and social-emotional support?
- ❏ Connect with these students in such a way that they are ready to learn?

Areas of Strength	Areas Where Growth Is Needed

How Do I Teach Them?

Guiding Questions: Do I (or we) . . .
- ❏ Implement instructional strategies and approaches that work for these students?
- ❏ Provide instruction that improves these students' reading, writing, and organization skills?
- ❏ Use information about these students' strengths and weaknesses to plan lessons and units that will meet their needs?

Areas of Strength	Areas Where Growth Is Needed

Tools 100 and 101: Action Plans

How Do I Keep the Bright Turned On?

Guiding Questions: Do I (or we) . . .

- ❑ Share what I (or we) have learned with others on behalf of students?
- ❑ Successfully advocate on behalf of students?
- ❑ Ensure that students develop the self-advocacy necessary for independence and success in the future?
- ❑ Help students learn and practice important life skills?
- ❑ Help students keep the bright turned on?

Areas of Strength	Areas Where Growth Is Needed

Tool 101: Action Plan Template

Directions: Use the template and your responses from Tool 100 to make a plan. Periodically update and record progress on the plan.

Area Where Growth is Needed	Desired State/ Goal	Action Steps	Timeline/Person Responsible	Progress Notes

Keeping the Bright Turned On

❑ **The Comment Book:** Create a simple booklet that can be set next to any student projects on display. Students and teachers in the school can make comments about the project, sharing their thoughts and compliments. (This idea was contributed by Joan Ridge.)

❑ **Project Ideas:** Once students have an opportunity to study a topic of their choice in depth, it often leads to their thinking of other projects or ideas that they want to explore. Encourage them to create a special place to keep their ideas for future study.

❑ **Pay It Forward: Mentee Becomes Mentor!** Once your student has had the chance of being mentored, encourage him or her to mentor a younger student.

❑ **Interest Clubs:** Encourage students with like interests to form a club in or out of school.

❑ **Guest Speakers:** Invite guest speakers to come to your class to expose students to different topics and perhaps spark their interest.

❑ **Authentic Audiences:** Equally as important as being involved in real-life problems is having authentic audiences with whom to share the findings. For example, seek out publications that print children's work, find contests for the budding photographer, connect the young scientist with a professional to discuss experiment findings, and so on.

❑ **Follow Their Passions:** Keep the spark lit by constantly searching for ways that your students can continue to develop their interests and pursue their dreams.

Resources for Teachers and Parents of Smart Kids With Learning Difficulties

2e (Twice-Exceptional) Newsletter—http://www.2enewsletter.com

All Kinds of Minds—http://www.allkindsofminds.org

Autism Society of America—http://www.autism-society.org

Children and Adults With Attention Deficit/Hyperactivity Disorder—http://www.chadd.org

Council for Exceptional Children—http://www.cec.sped.org

The Gifted With Learning Differences Educational Network—http://www.gtldnetwork.org

GreatSchools—http://www.greatschools.org/special-education.topic?content=1541

Hoagies' Gifted Education—http://www.hoagiesgifted.org

The International Dyslexia Association—http://www.interdys.org

LD Online—http://www.ldonline.org

Learning Disabilities Association of America—http://www.ldanatl.org

National Association for Gifted Children—http://www.nagc.org

National Center for Learning Disabilities—http://www.ncld.org

National Dissemination Center for Children With Disabilities—http://www.nichcy.org

NLD on the Web!—http://www.nldontheweb.org

Nonverbal Learning Disorders Association—http://www.nlda.org

Parent Encouragement Program—http://www.parentencouragement.org

Uniquely Gifted—http://www.uniquelygifted.org

U.S. Department of Education Office of Special Education and Rehabilitative Services—http://www.ed.gov/about/offices/list/osers/index.html

Wrightslaw Libraries—http://www.wrightslaw.com

Conclusion

What we share in common makes us human. How we differ
makes us individuals.

—Carol Ann Tomlinson

You have come to know Sarah, Jeremy, and Darryl as you followed them on their journeys from dependence to independence. Sarah has graduated from a strong liberal arts school and joined a marketing firm, where she works in a team and is highly respected for her creative ideas and verbal skills. Jeremy attended a small college where he was able to be in a supportive environment, studying computer programming. He is now working for a large information technology firm. Darryl graduated from an Ivy League school and received his degree in structural engineering. He is now working as an independent consultant. Given the right supports and opportunities to develop their talents and interests, the Sarahs, Jeremys, and Darryls of the world will become successful learners, going on to college and to successful careers.

Do you have students like Sarah, Jeremy, or Darryl, who have the capacity to change the world with the power of their thinking and the strength of their passion? If so, it is lucky for them that you are their teacher, as you now have the power of knowledge, an arsenal of tools, and the strength of your passion to remove the obstacles to allow for their personal, academic, and emotional growth. As an educator, you can feel the joy that comes from shaping and revealing the potential hidden within the student. You celebrate when your students realize their strengths, recognize themselves as capable learners, and develop their talents and interests, because this is when they begin to walk their path without you, and isn't that a wonderful thing?

References

Armstrong, T. (2000). *Multiple intelligences in the classroom* (2nd ed.). Alexandria, VA: Association for Supervision and Curriculum Development.

Barnes-Robinson, L., & Jeweler, S. (2007). *Conflict resolution: Teaching conflict resolution and mediation through the curriculum.* Hawthorne, NJ: Educational Impressions.

Barnes-Robinson, L., Jeweler, S., & Ricci, M. C. (2004). Potential: Winged possibilities to dreams realized! *Parenting for High Potential,* 20–25.

Barnes-Robinson, L., Jeweler, S., & Ricci, M. C. (2009, December). Pathways for developing potential in the social-emotional realm. *Parenting for High Potential,* 11–17.

Barton, J. M., & Starnes, W. T. (1989). Identifying distinguishing characteristics of gifted and talented/learning disabled students. *Roeper Review, 12*(1), 23–29.

Baum, S., Owen, S. V., & Dixon, J. (1991). *To be gifted and learning disabled.* Mansfield Center, CT: Creative Learning Press.

Brody, L. E., & Mills, C. J. (1997). Gifted children with learning disabilities: A review of the issues. *Journal of Learning Disabilities, 30,* 282–297.

Bruner, J. S. (1967). *On knowing: Essays for the left hand.* Cambridge, MA: Harvard University Press.

Cline, S., & Schwartz, D. (1999). *Diverse populations of gifted children.* Englewood Cliffs, NJ: Merrill/Prentice Hall.

Council for Exceptional Children. (2000). *Making assessment accommodations: A toolkit for educators.* Reston, VA: Author.

Dabrowski, K. (1964). *Positive disintegration.* Boston, MA: Little, Brown.

Dunn, R., Dunn, K., & Treffinger, D. (1992). *Bringing out the giftedness in your child: Nurturing every child's unique strengths, talents, and potential.* New York, NY: Wiley.

Fuchs, L. S., Fuchs, D., Eaton, S. B., Hamlett, C., & Karns, K. (2000). Supplementing teacher judgments about test accommodations with objective data sources. *School Psychology Review, 29*(1), 65–85.

Gardner, H. (1983). *Frames of mind: The theory of multiple intelligences.* New York, NY: Basic Books.

Gardner, H. (1993). *Multiple intelligences: The theory in practice.* New York, NY: Basic Books.

Higgins, D., Baldwin, L., & Pereles, D. (2000). *Comparison of characteristics of gifted students with or without disabilities.* Unpublished manuscript.

Individuals with Disabilities Education Act, PL-105, 111 Stat. 37 (1997).

Iseman, J. S., Silverman, S. M., & Jeweler, S. (2010). *101 school success tools for students with ADHD.* Waco, TX: Prufrock Press.

Levine, M. (2004). *The myth of laziness.* New York, NY: Free Press.

Maryland State Department of Education. (2000). *Requirements for accommodating, excusing, and exempting students in Maryland assessment programs.* Baltimore, MD: Author.

Montgomery County Public Schools. (2004). *Twice exceptional students: A guidebook for supporting the achievement of gifted students with special needs.* Rockville, MD: Author.

Morrison, W. F., & Rizza, M. G. (2007). Creating a toolkit for identifying twice-exceptional students. *Journal for the Education of the Gifted, 31,* 57–76.

National Association for Gifted Children. (1998). *Students with concomitant gifts and learning disabilities* (NAGC Position Paper). Washington, DC: Author.

National Association for Gifted Children. (2008). *Twice-exceptionality.* Retrieved from http://www.nagc.org/index.aspx?id=5094

Ogle, D. M. (1986). K-W-L: A teaching model that develops active reading of expository text. *Reading Teacher, 39,* 564–570.

Piechowski, M. M. (1991). *Emotional development and emotional giftedness.* In N. Colangelo & G. A. Davis (Eds.), *Handbook of gifted education* (pp. 285–306). Boston, MA: Allyn & Bacon.

Renzulli, J. S. (1977). *The enrichment triad model: A guide for developing defensible programs for the gifted and talented.* Mansfield Center, CT: Creative Learning Press.

Ricci, M. C., Barnes-Robinson, L., & Jeweler, S. (2006, September). Helping your children build on their visual-spatial strength in a world of words. *Parenting for High Potential,* 5–7, 30.

Section 504 of the Rehabilitation Act, 29 U.S.C. Section 706 et. Seq. (1973).

Shevitz, B., Weinfeld, R., Jeweler, S., & Barnes-Robinson, L. (2003). Mentoring empowers gifted/learning disabled students to soar. *Roeper Review, 26*(1), 37–40.

Thurlow, M., House, A., Scott, D., & Ysseldyke, J. (2001). *State participation and accommodation policies for students with disabilities.* Minneapolis, MN: National Center for Educational Outcomes.

Tomlinson, C. A. (1999). *The differentiated classroom: Responding to the needs of all learners.* Alexandria, VA: Association for Supervision and Curriculum Development.

Tomlinson, C. A. (2000). *Differentiation of instruction in the elementary grades.* Reston, VA: ERIC Clearinghouse on Disabilities and Gifted Education. (ERIC Document Reproduction Service No. ED443572)

Weinfeld, R., Barnes-Robinson, L., Jeweler, S., & Roffman Shevitz, B. (2006). *Smart kids with learning difficulties: Overcoming obstacles and realizing potential.* Waco, TX: Prufrock Press.

Zimmer, J. A. (1998). *Let's say: "We can work it out!" Problem solving through mediation, ages 8–13.* Culver City, CA: Social Studies School Service.

Authors' Note

The following tools were reprinted with permission from *Smart Kids With Learning Difficulties: Overcoming Obstacles and Realizing Potential* (Weinfeld et al., 2006): 4, 5, 12, 13, 30, 38, 40, 44, 45, 51, and 81.

The following tools were reprinted with permission from *101 School Success Tools for Students With ADHD* (Iseman et al., 2010): 48, 49, 64, 66, and 70.

About the Authors

Betty Roffman Shevitz has 30 years of experience with gifted students. She currently serves as an instructional specialist for gifted students in Montgomery County Public Schools (MCPS) and is responsible for the selection process for students to attend the Centers for the Highly Gifted in MCPS. In addition, she coordinates the Wings Mentor Program, which supports students who are both gifted and learning disabled. She has extensive experience both in the classroom and in the central office of school districts with large populations of gifted students. She has developed curriculum, presented at national and state conferences, and served as an educational consultant and a teacher trainer. She is coauthor of *Smart Kids With Learning Difficulties: Overcoming Obstacles and Realizing Potential* (2006) and two articles for *Roeper Review*. She received her bachelor's degree in education and her master's degree in gifted education from the University of Virginia.

Marisa Stemple has spent her entire career in education within Montgomery County Public Schools, working with and on behalf of bright students with learning difficulties. She began in 1997 as a teacher of gifted and talented/learning disabled (GT/LD) middle school students, before becoming the instructional specialist for GT/LD programs and services in 2004. She is responsible for coordinating MCPS' nationally recognized GT/LD programs. She also provides consultation and professional development on behalf of twice-exceptional students and works closely with the GT/LD Network, a parent advocacy group, to increase awareness and understanding of twice-exceptional students, programs, and services. She has presented at local, state, and national conferences on gifted education. She received her bachelor's degree in special education and her master's degree in learning disabilities from the

University of Maryland. She also received a certificate in administration and supervision from Johns Hopkins University.

Linda Barnes-Robinson has worked with children and parents for more than 30 years as a teacher and an advocate. With Montgomery County Public Schools, she coordinated the identification of gifted and talented students, advocated for parents and students, and worked to establish one of the first comprehensive programs for GT/LD students in the nation. Linda is a nationally recognized trainer and educational consultant in gifted identification, gifted/learning disabled programs, and conflict resolution education. She has coauthored and edited numerous books, articles, manuals, and curriculum documents, including her latest books, *Work Smart: In December the Forsythia Bloom, Teaching Conflict Resolution and Mediation Through the Curriculum,* and the best-selling *Smart Kids With Learning Difficulties: Overcoming Obstacles and Realizing Potential.* She received her master's degree from The George Washington University and a postgraduate certificate in family mediation from the Catholic University of America.

Sue Jeweler, a retired teacher, spent her 30-year career in Montgomery County Public Schools. Sue has been a consultant to the John F. Kennedy Center for the Performing Arts, the Smithsonian Institution, National Geographic, Berns & Kay, and Street Law. Her expertise has been used in a variety of projects with an outreach to teachers nationally and internationally. She has coauthored two educational kits, numerous journal articles, and more than 40 books, including the best-selling *Smart Kids With Learning Difficulties: Overcoming Obstacles and Realizing Potential* and *School Success for Kids With ADHD.* She has been the recipient of the prestigious *Washington Post* Agnes Meyer Outstanding Teaching Award. She coestablished Creative Family Projects, LLC, which identifies problems and provides solutions by synthesizing information from organizations, institutions, and corporations into booklets and training modules for the benefit of children, youth, and families.